GOOD MEDICINE: 100 Prayers from the Pandemic

Lessons on Loving, Connecting and Healing Through Spirit

Cecilia B. Loving

MYRTLE TREE PRESS

BROOKLYN, NEW YORK

Myrtle Tree Press LLC

Brooklyn, New York

https://www.amazon.com – Author's Page: Cecilia B. Loving

Good Medicine: 100 Prayers from the Pandemic:
Lessons on Loving, Connecting and Healing Through Spirit/
Cecilia B. Loving — First Edition

ISBN 978-1-7364224-0-3 (paperback) |

ISBN 978-1-7364224-1-0(ebook) |

Library of Congress Control Number: 2021909450

PRAISE for *GOOD MEDICINE*

"Cecilia is one of the most authentic and important spiritual teachers of our time! Her intentional words will reach deep within you and amplify the vibration of the frequency of love that is in you, and the love that is you.
Her daily nuggets of Wisdom and Truth inspire us to rise to new heights and embrace new levels of our personal greatness."
Rev. Randy Fikki, Founder, *I AM Spirit Creating*
Spiritual Director, Unity Southeast In Kansas City

"Cecilia Loving is a Spirit-filled expression of God.
Her words always find a place in the heart of others
to help them see themselves as spiritually able
to find their way in today's world.
This book speaks to this cosmic life experience
to give meaning and daily direction."
Rev. Carol J. Hunt, Unity in Harlem

"Transformative!
Faced with grief, fear, and confusion during the beginning of the pandemic, Cecilia Loving's prayers connected me to my sacred worth. Our prayers opened my heart to my divine purpose. Holding the light of rebirth, we began again..."
Jerome Smith, Member, Spiritmuv Church-in-Motion

"Cecilia Loving's latest offering *Good Medicine: 100 Days of Prayer During the Pandemic* is timely and will continue to be a staple for all of life's metaphoric pandemics as well as our battle with COVID-19. She challenges us to seek the holistic medicine of the Creator to heal and make us whole conscientious beings that sow into the very fabric of this global village. I implore everyone to get several copies, one for yourself and others to gift to those you desire to sow into."
Rev. Dr. Darryl Vaughn Footmon, Executive Pastor, Greenforest Community Baptist Church

"Cecilia, as her name implies, is very loving, and her love radiates in her work and service to others. She writes of all the profound Truth teachings and how to practically apply them through prayer and meditation to restore us to the wholeness that we are. This book is inspiring, practical, and so needed in our world today."
Rev. Eleanor Fleming, Unity Church Universal

"100 days of prayer is a reminder of many things. It reminds us of the consistency and faithfulness of our God. It reminds us of the power of presence when the women rise early in the morning to gather together. Miraculous things happen. Lastly, it is a reminder of the importance of prayer as our intimate language to thrive in our relationship with God and each other."
Rev. Dr. Leslie Duroseau, The God Factor

"Cecilia Loving has a name that speaks to her writing. She is loving and she has the uncanny ability to write in a very warm and loving way that not only calls us to task but also enlightens and embraces, warming our hearts to the point of surrender, and the reader can easily find themselves yielding to the over whelming and comforting ambiance of God. This book is sure to help the reader solidify and settle their 'being,' as they connect with the Spirit of unity and oneness and the reader will be at peace even during these most turbulent times."
Rev. Sandra Williams, Assistant Pastor, The Miracle Temple

"Thanks so much for so much during our Pandemic 100 Days of Prayer Reverend Cecilia B. Loving... I Know. I am reaping the blessings of the Kingdom. I am made brand new in a new heaven and new earth! So grateful for all the scriptures and lessons you blessed us with. THIS BOOK IS AMAZING!"
Paulette Lucas, One God, One Thought

"Loving has done it again! *Good Medicine* is like a breath of fresh air for spiritual fulfillment.
The prayers are thought provoking, uplifting and inspirational.
This book is timely in light of recent events. A must read!"
Elizabeth Walker, Member, Spiritmuv Church-in-Motion

"Cecilia's soul refreshing prayers speak to all hearts and minds in such an inspirational and moving way as we reimagine our post-pandemic lives.

Oh, what a blessing for such a time as this!"

Psalmist Sonya D. Johnson, Concord Baptist Church of Christ

"How do we operationalize our belief system to make a difference in our lives and the lives of our fellow members of the human race? Cecilia Loving's book *Good Medicine: 100 Days of Prayer* is foundational as a guide to move forward. We make the world better by taking the personal responsibility to be better. It is an outstanding read!"

Darsweil L. Rogers, Rogers Management Consultants

"During a time of great loss and uncertainty, *Good Medicine: 100 Days of Prayer During the Pandemic* serves as a reminder to focus on the things that matter most. This book will refocus your journey in faith and realign your feeling of oneness with God."

Bayliss Fiddiman, Member, Spiritmuv Church-in-Motion

For the memory of
those we lost during the pandemic,
including but not limited to
Catherine Werts,
Stan Williams,
Lori Dillon Sedia,
Suzanne Lynn,
Carlynn Stewart,
Richard Green,
James Paul Shivers,
Danny Kolenovic,
Anna Wiggins,
Elsa Rodriguez,
Sayed Rahman,
Brenda McKiver,
and everyone else
who allows us to stand
on their shoulders
and whose spirit girds us
with the pure love
of their souls.

Welcome to Good Medicine

For 100 days at the beginning of the 2020 pandemic, I got up every morning at 4:00 A.M., anxious about what was to come but determined to lead my church Spiritmuv's group of prayer warriors. When I awoke, I had no idea what I would say to start our prayers, but when I returned to the altar of grace each day, God gave me "good medicine" to share with others. We began praying for 40 days, what we call "as long as it takes." We had prayed together since 2014, every Saturday at 7:00 A.M., but this was something different. Our lives depended on the fortification of the Word to heal our bodies, minds, and souls, keep us centered in the power of something more magnificent than the physical, and provide us with the resilience we needed to move ahead. Our prayers were the source of such good medicine that by the time we got to the 100th day, I knew we could return to our weekly prayers. Even after we finished 100 days and no one was on the daily line, some would still call in, just to sit in the silence of such powerful vibrations.

We meditated and prayed, knowing that nothing is more powerful than God. The Holy Spirit guided me with lessons on the teachings of Jesus Christ, using the Bible (New International, American Standard, and New King James Versions), as well as other resources listed at the end of this book. You do not need to be of any particular faith to appreciate these lessons. They welcome everyone. We are all healers. We all have the power to bless ourselves and each other with good medicine.

No pandemic, politics, racism, economy, ego, election, or disease is greater than the kingdom of absolute good that resides in us and within which we live, move, and have our being. We awakened to the unknown, but also to the power of Spirit. We navigated a "new normal" and a revitalized faith in the gifts given to us as children of God.

With people suffering and dying everywhere, locked in, and locked out, racial tensions heightened as the world suddenly opened its eyes and saw knees on the necks of bodies racialized as black and brown. We listened more carefully to Ibram X. Kendi, Ta-Nehisi Coates, Isabel Wilkerson, Robin Di Angelo, Reesma Menakem, Rhonda Magee, Sharon Salzberg, Ruth King, and others who reminded us we are all connected. We began to solve problems "above the level of the problem," that is, above the toxic vibrations that created them. Together, we lifted ourselves above the fray, and in that awareness, we found Spirit.

These are the lessons that focused our prayers. Read the prayer lesson for each day in chronological order, or select one randomly. These words are just part of the energy that opened our hearts to the "good medicine" that is always within our souls.

Reverend Cecilia B. Loving

Acknowledgments

For the Spiritmuv Prayer Warriors who spent 100 days together in
our virtual prayer circle every morning at 7:00 A.M.,
from March 15, 2020, to June 21, 2020, during the first few months
of the COVID-19 pandemic,
Mother Myrtle Ross,
Rev. Marlon Cromwell,
Elizabeth Walker,
Latanya Wilson,
Alma Ferrell,
Deidre Sheffield,
Jerome Smith,
Sabrina Griffin,
Paulette Lucas,
Timothy Smith,
Lynette Williams,
Fern Rankin,
Charlotte Brown,
Donna Jones,
Bernadette Burgess,
Vanessa Hendon,
Sandra Hancock,
Sonya Thomas,
Cheryl Turner,
Kennet Sampson Griffin,
Abayomi Ajaiyeoba Whint, and Eunice Ajaiyeoba,
Yvonne Shivers,
Chaplain Robinson, ,
and everyone else whose presence will always be part of
our circle of prayer.

Contents

I AM Greater Than Before

It's time to own our greatness.

Matthew 19:16-17 says someone came to Jesus and asked Him, "Good Teacher, what good thing shall I do that I may have eternal life?" Jesus said to the man, why do you call me good? No one is good, but One who is God. If you want to have eternal life, keep the commandments. As we pray, we keep the Commandments in our hearts, especially the Third Commandment, which says, "[y]ou shall not take the name of the Lord your God in vain, for the Lord will not hold him guiltless who takes His name in vain" (Exodus 20:7). But what exactly does that mean?

I used to think that the Third Commandment meant you could not say a curse word, especially one with God's name in it. However, the Third Commandment goes a lot deeper, raising the question: *what are you saying about the power in you?* "Vain" is a mistranslation. The Aramaic root wood is *dagalootha*, which means falsehood, suggesting that the commandment reads, "[y]ou shall not take the name of the Lord your God falsely." In other words, Spirit, God, Absolute Good, Divine Mind, the Universe, Unlimited Source, whatever you call the "Most High," should never undermine the spiritual integrity of God as the only power there is. I use a variety of words to refer to God. I especially love "Spirit" because it requires that we imagine God as something more expansive than an old man in the sky.

In Luke 12:32, Jesus said, "it is your Father's good pleasure to give you the Kingdom." Have you opened your consciousness to receive it? Or have you used your words to deny its existence? Are you speaking words that remind you that you are God's image and likeness? Or do you insist on bad-mouthing the Kingdom of Absolute Good in you? What are you telling yourself? Do you realize there is too much power in Spirit to bless you with anything less than the greatness that you are? Do you see yourself as "I AM WHO I AM," the image and likeness of Spirit? Have you stopped second-guessing the power within you?

Moses second-guessed himself. He asked, who am I to lead the people? I cannot even speak well. Yet, God revealed that Moses had all he needed to lead the Israelites, aided by the power of Spirit. All Moses needed to do was tell the Israelites that "I AM

WHO I AM" sent him (Exodus 3:14), which Jesus taught us was the name of his own indwelling Spirit (John 14:17).

Moses learned that every single thought, word, or utterance is speaking truth to power. We should not refer to ourselves in a manner that undermines our greatness. When we marginalize ourselves, we marginalize the power of God expressing as us.

We all have "a negativity bias." Scientists have established that we all speak negative monologues to ourselves, doubting ourselves, frustrating our potential, complaining about our past, worrying about our futures, questioning God's blessings for us, instead of realizing the divine potential within. We can demonstrate our good right now. We can mold, shape, and express our joy right now. We can co-create with a universe of endless possibilities right now.

Jesus says in Matthew 12:36 that you shall give an account on judgment day for every careless word that you utter. Judgment Day is every day. Judgment Day is the period of reaping what we sow in everything we think, say, or do. When we participate in a pity party about how we don't have anyone, how we haven't done what we intended to do, or how we didn't receive our due—we are taking the Lord's name in vain. When we dwell in the negative, we give power to it.

Whatever we decree shall be established (Job 22:28 ASV). If we are "poor-mouthing," claiming poverty regardless of what we have, then we give power to poverty. If we dwell on illness, we stay sick. If we keep thinking about bad relationships, we manifest them. If we focus on insecurity, loneliness, or lack, we establish them. If we dwell on failure, we decree it.

Now is the time to speak truth to power, acknowledge the greatness within, stop seeing the glass as half full, realize our table is prepared before our enemies. We can stop thinking and talking about loss, denial, rejection, lack, limitation, and worry, and instead say victory is my name. My water is walked. My sores are healed. My demons have fled. My vision is restored. My ship is in. My season has arrived. My goodness is seeking me. My divine opportunity and abundance are blessing me right now.

Every challenge opens a portal to be made brand new—to stop stressing, judging, and undermining ourselves. We can acknowledge here and now: "I AM A CHILD OF GOD, HEIR TO THE THRONE OF INFINITE GOOD. I DO NOT WORSHIP MAN AS THE SOLE SOURCE OF MY GOOD BECAUSE HUMANITY IS LIMITED. MY GOOD DOES NOT STEM FROM ONE JOB, EMPLOYER, PERSON, RELATIONSHIP, EVENT, OUTCOME, OPPORTUNITY, PROJECT, GOAL, OR ACHIEVEMENT. I DO NOT LOOK AT THE SOURCE OR JUDGE THE SUPPLY BECAUSE GOD'S BLESSINGS ARE INEXHAUSTIBLE."

I decree absolute good in my life here and now.

Gratitude Pushes Me Past Present to God

It's time to realize that God is not limited by past, present, or future.

When I awoke this morning, the Holy Spirit gave me the law of gratitude, a principle that I had not focused on before as spiritual law. Spiritual law guarantees the outcome we desire, consciously or unconsciously. *Spiritual law provides us with a way to navigate the human to trust in the divine.* As spiritual law, gratitude pushes us past our present circumstances to tap the full flow of inexhaustible supply that we call abundance, which is God everywhere present.

Gratitude not only praises what we know but also uplifts what we do not know. We can praise God for what we have, but also for those blessings that have yet to manifest. We can be grateful for our good, even before it shows up. We can wake up and say, "God, you have blessed me with air to breathe and space to take up and the pure grace of being your child, your daughter, your son in whom you are well-pleased. I am grateful for your presence and how you carry us through each moment."

We should not limit ourselves to relying on an external reality to make us feel different. Instead, we can give thanks before the manifestation of the good that we seek. Give thanks and feel the power of your gratitude already bringing forth that for which you give thanks. We should move from cause and effect. Cause and effect is change because of something you did, but change is not always caused by what we do.

Gratitude also impacts our experiences. The more often we express, experience, and generate the energy of gratitude, the more great-filled experiences we have. But when we give our attention to what we don't want, the reverse is true. We must be careful about the vibrations we send because the universe does not know the difference between what we want and what we don't want. Using positive affirmations can diffuse the negative energy of careless thoughts and the lower vibrations of undesired outcomes. We must remain diligent so we do not unknowingly embrace the negative energy of those around us.

We believe getting material things is important, but changing our consciousness to realize that we are one with the Kingdom of God is the ultimate goal. If we are one with God's Kingdom, then we know our good is always here. The way we think co-creates our experiences. It is better to realize our power as children of Spirit, which will always manifest our greatest good. By being grateful, we will not only experience more gifts that we have to be grateful for, but we will also develop more ways to express our gratitude. When we change our perception from a negative one (the world is inherently unfair) to a better one (my good is manifesting), *we change what we are grateful for in our hearts to what we experience in the world.*

Matthew 14:19 says that Jesus took the five loaves and two fish and, looking up to heaven, "he gave thanks" and broke the loaves. He acknowledged the endless flow of abundance in Spirit before it multiplied. A grateful heart opens the door to the flow and becomes an attractive force to draw the great things already there. Let us be thankful for all of our blessings, including *those blessings that have not yet taken shape in the physical realm.*

Let us pour gratitude into the universe, to Divine Mind, to God, to the spiritual ethers, to the quantum realm, to everywhere and nowhere, and know that beyond this time-space-dimension, our good has already manifested. Perhaps there are some things, blessings, shifts, healings, or guidance you desire without praying for them because you could not imagine them manifesting. Let us turn those unspoken prayers into thoughts of gratitude right now.

We cannot envision many inventions involving technology, events, and circumstances not yet encountered, so we need the broader vision of the Universe to manifest our greatest good. Let us be grateful now and align ourselves with the unseen, forming and shaping for our best. One thing that we do know is that the universe is always conspiring to bless us. We believe we are not worthy to receive so many things, but gratitude humbles us and encourages us to see past our presumed limitations to God's greatness.

Let us feel, trust, and know that whatever we desire is already done, already a praise report, already a win, already a miracle. Even those things that may have appeared to be injustices, setbacks, lies, the work of the devil, the result of haters, someone who meant us evil—are all part of God's plan to bless us. The Father-Mother-Everything-Almighty-Heavenly God never stops manifesting our good.

Gratitude is not limited to a place, thing, person, or situation; it is energy aligned with the flow of absolute good. With gratitude, there is a connection with the love that is everywhere present, just waiting to bless us. With gratitude, we move beyond desire and open our hearts to receive the unlimited flow of good: a good that is so great we cannot even name it.

I decree gratitude for the blessings of the unseen.

Faith Muscles Improve When They Are Tested

It's time to work out our faith muscles.

There is never a better time to learn than when we are tested. Tests are the times that we fortify our resilience. Tests remind us to build community, care for each other, make the world a better place, and develop new habits that serve us better than the old ones. Either we confront the negative or embrace the positive when we have challenges. We can fret, freeze, fight, fear, or we can trust, realizing that our faith muscles only improve when tested. Paul said, "[d]o not conform to the pattern of this world, but be transformed by the renewing of your mind. Then you will be able to test and approve what God's will is—his good, pleasing and perfect will" (Romans 12:2). He said, "[w]hen we have learned not to give up, it shows we have stood the test. When we have stood the test, it gives us hope" (Romans 5:4).

Every test is an opportunity to change. The Book of James teaches us in the 1st Chapter, Verses 2-4, to "consider it pure joy" whenever you face trials of any kind. The testing of our faith produces perseverance. We must let perseverance finish its work so that we may be "mature and complete, not lacking anything."

Similarly, 1 Chronicles 4: 10 is where Jabez cried, "Oh, that you would bless me and enlarge my territory! Let your hand be with me and keep me from harm so that I will be free from pain." We know that God granted his request and solidified our faith with the wisdom that we, too, will be blessed when we trust in God. We realize the power of God through the demonstration of our tests. When tested, our good rewards, restores, revitalizes, and rejuvenates us in ways we could never imagine.

Triumph is often a teachable moment. We receive rewards beyond our comprehension. We receive gifts beyond what we have requested. We receive guidance we had no idea was available. When tested, we learn that our capacity to receive God's grace is directly in response to our willingness to give our trust in one source: Spirit.

I decree my faith is perfected with every test.

Everything Comes Together for Our Greatest Good

It's time to trust that God has our back.

The book of Matthew, the Eighth Chapter, Verses 5-13, tells the story of a Centurion, a commander of the Roman army, who went to Jesus and told him that *one of his servants was extremely ill*, lying home paralyzed. Jesus offered to heal him. But the Centurion said, no, I am not worthy of having you come under my roof, and I have soldiers awaiting my command. I trust that you can merely speak a word, and he will be healed.

The Centurion was saying: I understand the power of commands because I order people all day. All you have to do is give a command, and I know that the forces of the universe will carry out your wishes. Jesus was surprised by the Centurion's faith and said to him: "Go! Let it be done just as you believed it would." The scripture teaches us that the Centurion's servant "was healed at that moment" (Matthew 8:13).

Trust, and you will find that everything comes together for your greatest good. Trust in the unlimited power and presence of Spirit that is always available to you. Trust your wisdom. Trust your creativity. Trust that you have the power to co-create with the quantum realm of absolute good with a Spirit of fearlessness and a conviction so strong that you need not worry about the appearances of things.

When we fail to trust that God has our back, we diminish our power. Imagine what would have happened if Jesus listened to someone who said he could not multiply fish and bread. Imagine what would have happened if Jesus listened to the disciples' fear about the wind and the waves as he was about to walk on water. Imagine what would have happened if Jesus was about to heal the sick, make the lame walk, or help the blind see, but he was influenced by non-believers who said there is no way they could be healed.

Imagine what would have happened if the woman with the issue of blood listened to someone who said, "hey wait a minute, you know, you're just pushing through a crowd to touch a man's garment." Imagine what would have happened if Jesus, who was crucified, dead and buried, did not rely on the omnipotent, omniscient, omnipresence of the God in him and chose to join all those other people who said, "he ain't gonna rise again." Rather than trust naysayers, we should trust the presence and power of God in us. We will not recognize the gifts and talents that God gave us if we are too busy factoring in what other people think, or wasting time on what *we think* they think.

Go thy way as thou hast believed, Jesus said, and so be it done unto thee. Be lifted in the truth that Spirit has taught you. Chart your course. Step into the vortex of your creative consciousness, and trust that you can give your best to those around you. Are you just bemoaning a fate that someone else is creating for you because you gave them your power, instead of co-creating with divine source that has no limit?

Ralph Waldo Emerson said, "[t]o believe your own thought, to believe that what is true for you in your private heart is true for all...that is genius.... In every work of genius we recognize our own rejected thoughts: they come back to us with a certain alienated majesty." If we do not trust the voice of Spirit guiding us, then we will sacrifice the gift of God's divine ideas. "Trust thyself: every heart vibrates to that iron string.... Nothing is at last sacred but the integrity of your own mind. ... What I must do is all that concerns me, not what the people think," Emerson said.

Trust the divine ideas that you are given. Trust the infinite possibilities that await you. Trust your voice to speak truth to power. Trust your ability to step outside of the box of convention and be the world differently—be better, create more, bless beyond, uplift higher, express endlessly, manifest miracles, grow greatness, stop worrying about what someone else thinks and shine the light that you are—the air that you breathe and the space that you take up, and the unlimited love of the universe's expression as you.

I decree that Spirit guides me here and now.

We Can Elevate Our Emotions to be Complete in Joy

It's time to make our joy complete.

When we open our hearts to elevated emotions like joy, happiness, adoration, appreciation, and praise, we improve our immune system. We change our biology from living in the past to being in the now. We go from selfish states to selfless states. Ten minutes of joyful thoughts boost our immune system. But ten minutes of anger, frustration, impatience, or fear turns on 1200 different chemicals that suppress our immune system. Where you place your attention is where you place your energy. The moment joy moves into our hearts, the field around our body expands rather than diminishes from negative vibrations. When our energy field shrinks, it lowers our immune system. Living in survival mode diminishes our immunity because we trigger the stressors of fight, flight, or fright.

We want to be in the vortex of elevated emotions that draw what we need to us. We can trust the unknown, trust that we are part of the absolute good of the Kingdom of God, and the universe conspires to help rather than to defeat us. Right here, right now, at this moment, each one of us has the potential for joy, and the only question is, how do we want to experience it? In Psalm 51:12, the Psalmist says, "[r]estore to me the joy of your salvation and grant me a willing spirit, to sustain me." We can elevate our emotions to be receptive to God's restorative powers.

Jeremiah said, "When your words came, I ate them; they were my joy and my heart's delight, for I bear your name, Lord God Almighty" (Jeremiah 15:16). In John 16:24, Jesus says, "[u]ntil now you have not asked for anything in my name. Ask, and you will receive, and your joy will be complete." I joyously speak the name of Jesus, and I ask and receive God's joy. In Philippians 2:2, Paul says, "make my joy complete by being like-minded, having the same love, being one in spirit and of one mind." I take joy in the Divine Mind of God, knowing that it not only comforts me but it co-creates joy in all of my experiences. I call it all "joy."

I decree that I am complete in the joy of Spirit.

My Life is in Perfect, Divine Order

It's time to be at peace with divine order.

In 2 Chronicles, Chapter 34, Verses 1-2, it says, "Josiah was eight years old when he began to reign as King, and he reigned thirty and one years in Jerusalem." Josiah did what was right in the eyes of Jehovah; when he was 12 years old, he purged Judah and Jerusalem. The scripture says he "did what was right in the eyes of the Lord and followed the ways of his father David, not turning aside to the right or the left." He was focused.

Josiah means whom Jehovah supports. Josiah represents our ability to be committed and honest enough to do what is necessary to be pure in the Spirit. We get rid of our unnecessary stuff. We let go of our past. We cleanse, de-clutter, throw away, give away whatever is not for our highest good. Spiritual teacher Denise Linn calls de-cluttering the "alchemy" of the Spirit. The deeper and more in-depth the cleansing, the more powerful our focus, clarity, and demonstration of perfect, divine order.

We depart from one dwelling place to go to a new and better one. We lose part of our team but attract new team members who are even stronger and more supportive and loving than ever before. We lose our job, but we get one that pays more and is so much better. We re-locate and find ourselves in the best place possible to experience the manifestation of our desires.

In Psalm 119, the 133rd Verse, the Psalmist says, order my steps according to Your Word. Order is the divine connection to the Holy Spirit's guidance, which directs us from limited to unlimited source. When we put God first, we do not have to worry about the appearances of things because we can trust that perfect divine order is blessing us with what we need when we need it.

We can trust that everything will happen in perfect divine order. We examine our lives and realize that everything that happened was for the best. Sometimes, I often laugh out loud when I look back and see that even when it appeared that someone meant something for evil, God meant it for good (Genesis 50:20). Even when someone intends to hurt us, their actions become a catalyst to manifest our good. Even attacks can catapult us into a higher realm of consciousness that focuses our energy on God, sharpening our commitment to center in the only power that there is. The more devious and intentional, the more an attack adds to our favor—if we do not lower ourselves to the negative vibrations but stay lifted in the energy of pure love.

Nothing and no one stands in the way of our good. Order creates clarity so that when Spirit tells us to do something, we do it, and the things we desire manifest with ease. I exercise my power of Order, and God tells me where to go and what to do, and everything falls into place. I need to write a paper, but there is no time in the physical: books nearly fall off the shelves, giving me exactly what I need. When I use my power of order, I know that there is no end to God's good.

A divine plan is unfolding through you now. You have a magnificent purpose on this planet earth, and your realization of this purpose is ordering your life in a special way. In the 37th Psalm, the Psalmist says the 23rd Verse, "[t]he steps of a good man are *ordered* by the Lord." In God's order, there is no limitation as to time, space, or means because God is pure potential, infinite waves of possibility without beginning or end. We cannot see the complete picture, so we are still and know that our affairs are ordered by divine intelligence.

Order takes place instantly—beyond time, or space, or body; order is always in the outworking of our affairs. It might take a while to appear on the outer, but it begins with your first acceptance of order. God, I put You first in my continuous development beyond all appearances. I know that Your Divine Order governs my life, every step I take, and every word I utter. I know there are no coincidences, that no weapon formed against me prospers. Ways are already being made out of no way; doors that I need have already opened; answers that I sought are being revealed. What I have asked for—I have already been given. I am perfect, whole, and well in Your Spirit. All obstacles have been moved out of my way.

I decree that my steps are in perfect divine order.

I Reap the Blessings of the Kingdom

It's time to reap the benefits of the Kingdom.

In John 4: 35-38, Jesus tells his disciples, "Do you not say, 'Four months more and then the harvest'? I tell you, open your eyes and look at the fields! They are ripe for harvest. Even now the reaper draws his wages, even now he harvests the crop for eternal life, so that the sower and the reaper may be glad together. Thus, the saying 'One sows and another reaps' is true. I sent you to reap what you have not worked for. Others have done the hard work, and you have reaped the benefits of their labor." Today, right now, is the day to reap the blessings of the Kingdom.

We are all connected with one another. Despite the appearance of being alone and isolated, we are all part of the same harvest. Our future does not rest on one person, leader, or messiah with a greater consciousness to show us the way. Instead, it requires the evolution of a new collective consciousness. Through the interconnectedness of human consciousness, we can reap our good and change the course of history. While it appears old structures and paradigms are collapsing, we should not face this with fear, anger, or sadness because this is the process by which evolution and necessary changes take place. Instead, we should face the future with new wisdom, energy, and consciousness that the old falls away so something new can flourish.

I reap a kingdom beyond pandemonium, pandemic, and panic where there is a wealth of vaccinations, healings, and manifestations in science that will bless, re-connect and strengthen us. Paul told the Corinthians in 2 Corinthians 9:8-11, "God is able to make all grace abound to you, so that in all things at all times, having all that you need, you will abound in every good work. [God] increases your store of seed and will enlarge the harvest of your righteousness."

I reap the prosperity of endless manna. My harvest is plentiful. The universe keeps blessing me with what some would call miracles, but I know it as my divine inheritance.

I decree that this is my season.

I am Made New

It's time to be made new.

In 2 Corinthians 5:16-17, Paul says, "[e]ven though we have known Christ according to the flesh, yet now we know Him thus no longer. Therefore, if anyone is in Christ, he is a new creation; old things have passed away; behold, all things have become new." When I think of newness, I cannot help but think of John 3:3, when Nicodemus snuck out in the middle of the night and went to Jesus for his counsel, saying, I know you must be a teacher from God. Jesus tells Nicodemus that he must be born again—unless one is born again, he cannot see the kingdom of God. Not reborn from the womb but from water and Spirit.

In Acts 2:13, when the day of Pentecost came, and people of Spirit from around the world began speaking in tongues, they could all understand the wonderful works of God, but those mocking them said, "[t]hey are full of new wine." They were filled with new wine, but not the kind of wine the mockers understood. What was this new wine? 1 Corinthians 11:25 reminds us that Jesus "took the cup after supper, saying, 'This cup is the new covenant in My blood. This, do, as often as you drink it, in remembrance of Me.'" The new wine is the new covenant, the embodiment of Christ consciousness in us.

Are we capable of pouring this new wine into our old experiences? Have we returned from the "far country" of excess and debauchery? Are we lifted in the enlightenment of new skins, or are we still stuck in old habits? Are we still tied to the despair of our former selves? Do we believe in the words and teachings of Jesus, directing us to put on the new self to know that we must judge by righteous judgment rather than by mere appearances?

When we study truth, it does not teach us fear. Truth teaches us the boldness of prayer. The boldness of prayer is knowing that we can ask and receive: the boldness of not worrying but seeking first the kingdom, the boldness of casting our nets on the right side and hauling in more than we can lift, the boldness of realizing that we are in the Father and Jesus is in us, the boldness of the greater things that we are here to do. As Jesus walks with us, he is not separate from us. The consciousness of Christ dwells within us and will turn what we see in the flesh into new wine.

In Matthew 9:17, Jesus says: "they don't put new wine into old wineskins, or else the wineskins break, the wine is spilled, and the wineskins are ruined. But they put new wine into new wineskins, and both are preserved." How do we put the new wine that

Jesus has anointed us with into our old thoughts of fear, our old thoughts of worry, our old thoughts of sickness, our old thoughts of lack? We release the negativity, and we do as Romans 7:6 says, "we serve in the newness of the Spirit and not in the oldness of the letter."

We have been made new, and in our newness, we can stop begging God out of a state of fear. We are praying to believe with new strength, new wisdom, new light, so we are born again in the new wisdom, the new light, the new truth, the new word of Jesus filling our bodies, our minds, our words, and our souls with new vision, new awareness, new power, new strength, new wine.

Are you walking with the presence of Christ in you—your hope of glory? Will you cower and fret? Will you doubt and fear? Or will you send the white light of healing power—that is always available to you throughout the world? Will you tap into and turn on the absolute grace of God and send healing strength to the unseen, resilience to the health care providers, courage to the front line? Will you decree with the Spirit of new wine and be reborn in the kingdom within?

When I think of new wine, I am reminded of an ancient Tibetan Buddhist practice. When there was a pandemic of leprosy in Tibet, they used Tonglen. Tong means giving or sending, and len means receiving or taking. We breathe in sickness, pain, suffering, negativity, doubt, despair—by starting with ourselves, and as this despair enters our body through the nose and settles in our heart, our healing center of love purifies all fear, sickness, and disease—healing and purifying us from within. Then, we breathe out, positive energy, joy, wisdom, and purity stream from our heart as light towards all beings.

Jesus says to me, I have given you the ability to lay on hands through the heart and mind and soul of who you are. Come with me to the altar of light and breathe in the pandemic, breathe in pandemonium, breathe in pain, breathe in suffering, breathe in sickness, breathe in fear, agitation, anger, resistance—*and breathe out light, love, truth, compassion, kindness.* Our hearts and souls can change from old to new. Breathe out new wine that transforms the appearance of sickness, poison, hatred, fear, resentment into good medicine. Use the power of Spirit as the ultimate alchemy to breathe renewal into the lives of everyone, and in this synergy, let us be made brand new.

I decree a new wine of wholeness.

I Release and Let Go

It's time to release and let go.

The Book of Matthew, the Fifth Chapter, the 29-30th Verses say, "if your right eye causes you to stumble, gouge it out and throw it away. It is better for you to lose one part of your body than for your whole body to be thrown into hell. And if your right hand causes you to stumble, cut it off and throw it away. It is better for you to lose one part of your body than for your whole body to go into hell." This release and letting go is the deliverance of our power of renunciation: the power to cleanse, to de-clutter, to eliminate negativity, to lower vibrations, to remove blockages to our good. Renouncing what is not for our highest good and letting it go opens space for what we desire to manifest. When we do not release, we allow the toxins of what we do not want or need to harden and calcify, and the ability to move forward becomes more difficult—just like the residue in a pipe.

Remember Lot's wife? As her family was fleeing from Sodom and Gomorrah, symbolic of decadence being cleansed by God, Lot and his family (who escaped) were told not to look back. But Lot's wife looked back, and she "became a pillar of salt" (Genesis 19:26). Salt is a preservative, corresponding to keeping or preserving something in *status quo*. When we keep hanging onto the past, we stagnate ourselves. We, too, turn into pillars of salt.

Perhaps it is the blockage of old habits, old traits, old stories that we have locked ourselves into, or the spaces around us are so full of stuff that it binds us to the past. Cleansing in the physical aids what needs to happen in the spiritual. Let go of the representation of those things in your environment that are stuck in the past—not only those things you do not need but also those that represent areas and people and events you need to release. When we clean our living and work environments, we open new space in our lives and affairs.

What is there that you need to release and let go of to forgive others? It can be more difficult to hold on to that which we falsely believe still serves us because of our need to define ourselves by it. Because of our pride, we want to hold on to a past that no longer exists. Because of our unwillingness to part from those stories or complaints that we have carried for so long that we cannot imagine ourselves without them, we live in the past.

I remember when I left a firm where I worked for 20 years. I threw away everything with the firm's name on it, which was a process because I had about 15 boxes delivered from my office. I enjoyed my experience at the firm, but it was important for me to move forward without confining how I defined myself solely to that experience.

If there are financial issues, throw away those things that steep you in that consciousness of lack. Generally, you can destroy receipts and statements that are older than seven years.

We sometimes need to process how to let go of previous experiences, especially those that trigger us. When we are holding onto negativity, we get stuck in its lower vibration. What we condemn in others is what we condemn in ourselves. Let it go. Forgive the past and liberate yourself. Any harboring of resentment chains us to yesterday—stagnates us like Lot's wife. Compassion frees us.

As one of my poems in my recent book *Unbroken Circles* says, "hold the circle open for Lot's wife." She is that part of us that sometimes needs others to hold space for us so we can process what needs releasing. We all need help sometimes.

Let us bless anything stuck in the past, even ourselves. Say, "I bless you to yourselves; I bless you and forgive you for whatever you did not do or were powerless to perform, for whatever hurt you or attempted to destroy you, for whatever you tried but were unsuccessful in releasing, for whatever kept you stuck." You can now move on. I release and let go of anyone and anything that no longer serves my highest good; whatever there is in the flesh that I cannot release, I put at the altar of God's grace so that Spirit can do the work for me.

I let go of all erroneous beliefs, all fears, all jealousies, all doubts, all dis-ease, all pain. I release their hold over me and generations to come. I release the discord of my suffering, my hurt, as well as the sins and deep trauma of our ancestors, regardless of their ethnicity (be they black, brown, red, yellow, or white). I release the hurt and sorrow and misery carried in our bones.

I let go of the pain that has emerged as a pandemic, and I accept the light and restoration of its anti-bodies, of its natural restorative healing. I am renewed today. I am restored in the light of renunciation. I empty all my baggage today, every false belief, every grain of salt that once held me suspended in a state of disbelief, and I enter a new space of consciousness, a new light of understanding, a new vibrancy of wholeness.

I decree the release of whatever and whoever no longer serves my greatest good.

I Celebrate My Life

It's time to celebrate every year of my life.

In his book *The Science of Self-Empowerment: Awakening the New Human Story*, the scientist and mystic Gregg Braden shares the story of Li Ching-Yuen, a Chinese martial artist and qigong master. Ching-Yuen did not only live a good long life—but he did for *256 years*. I did not say he was 256 "years old"; that is what we Americans would say. *I said after living for 256 years.*

According to Braden, Ching-Yuen was born in China in 1677; he retired at 97. The military records show that they congratulated him three times: on his 100th birthday, his 150th birthday, and, in 1877, on his 200th birthday. He made his transition 56 years later, in 1933. At the time of his death, records credit him with 180 children from 14 marriages. When asked about the secret of his longevity, Ching-Yuen said the secret to a long life is to "have a quiet heart."

Braden also shares the story of a nun he met, who was showing him around and had a special title usually reserved for monks. She had lived for 120 years. Unlike others, her age records were preserved in the monastery's library. When Braden asked her about the secret to her longevity, she said it was compassion: "Compassion is life. It's what we practice here. It's what we learn from our masters and what they learn from theirs."

Do you believe that you begin to die from the moment you are born, or do you accept that our birth triggers the healing process that is natural and inherent to continue our existence? I would not say that I am "so many years old," but that *"x" number of years has passed since I came into this life.*

The late Eric Butterworth used to teach us that the only reason we die of natural causes is because we have programmed ourselves into believing that it is part of the natural course of life. What if you knew that most people lived to 256 years old: Would you dwell on arthritis or other so-called age-related ailments? Have you seized the fullness of life? Let's strip away our notions of what we are used to and rise in the synergy of what is: we are supernatural healers with the power of a loving heart that heals every sickness that cures the appearance of every dis-ease. We are supernatural agents of life who are ageless beings of light, love, wholeness, and grace.

I decree youth no matter how old I am.

I Have Divine Vision

It's time to see beyond appearances.

On the third day, when God said let the dry land appear, the ancient text uplifts the visualization of Creative Consciousness, of the eyes of God—seeing beyond lack to abundance, seeing beyond limitation to unlimited greatness, seeing beyond appearances to infinite good seeing beyond worry to a confident realization that whatever needs to take shape is already manifesting.

Our power of divine vision—letting the dry land appear, the earth beneath our feet, the shape and form of our blessings remind me of the Book of John, the 9th Chapter, Verses 1-12, when Jesus was traveling with his disciples and "[h]e saw a man who was blind from birth. And his disciples asked him, 'Rabbi, who sinned, this man or his parents, that he was born blind?' 'Neither this man nor his parents sinned,' said Jesus, 'but this happened so that the work of God might be displayed in his life.'" Having said this, Jesus spit on the ground, made some mud with the saliva, and put it on the man's eyes. "'Go,' he told him, 'wash in the Pool of Siloam.' So, the man went and washed, and came home seeing. His neighbors and those who had formerly seen him begging asked, 'Isn't this the same man who used to sit and beg?'" Some claimed that he was, but others said, 'No, he only looks like him.' But he insisted, 'I am the man.' 'How then were your eyes opened?' How, then, can you see? And the man replied, 'The man they call Jesus made some mud and put it on my eyes. He told me to go to Siloam and wash. So I went and washed, and then I could see. 'I once was blind, but now I see.'"

When we read this story, we get so caught up with what we call a miracle that we lose sight of its fundamental message: the power of sight, the power of vision, the power of seeing beyond the flesh to the manifestation of our good is always available to us.

In the story of the creation, the third day blesses us with divine vision. Divine vision is the co-creative power to open our eyes, hearts, and souls to see past appearances. As John 7:24 says, judge not by appearances but realize the power within. Stop being blind to the truth that as children of God, we can co-create with the inexhaustible Spirit of Absolute Good and make a way out of no way.

We can wash in the pool of Siloam—go and cleanse our vision of false ideas, see past violence to peace, see beyond hatred to solidarity, see past fear to trust. We can open our eyes and see the divine in us.

When we read the book of Genesis (Chapters 5-6), we see that Noah's spiritual vision allowed him to be warned of things not yet seen and that he prepared an ark according to his faith and through his preparation and obedience, he was saved. We see that Abraham's spiritual vision allowed him to see the new place—the new country where God called him to receive his blessings (Genesis 22). We see that Jacob's spiritual vision allowed him to free himself from his father-in-law's land to become one of the richest men alive and to free him from his brother's wrath so that he could live in peace (Genesis 31). Jacob's vision uplifts his faith—the evidence of things unseen.

The "projected diary" is a tool that we can use to activate our power of divine vision; it is mentioned in Eric Butterworth's book *The Creative Life*. I have used it in the past, and it works. One of the ways that I used the projected diary is for mental and physical strength. For example, I wanted to do un-assisted pull-ups, but I could not. I struggled for months, and my trainer Goss would spot me. One morning, I was on my way to the gym, and I decided to use the projected diary. I wrote: "Today, I do unassisted pull-ups." When I arrived at the gym, I did not just do one, but I did three sets of eight un-assisted pull-ups!

We can use the projected diary's power whenever we need to see past where we fall short, where we feel lack, where we are out of control, where we keep missing the mark. The projected diary is one of infinite ways that we can use our power of divine vision.

~ 35 ~

Another tool to see past what we cannot do and realize what God can do is write a letter to the day, the week, the month, or even the year before it takes place. We can create a vision board of drawings and photographs of what we would like to take place. Anything that allows us to create what we would like to experience envisions dry land emerging, good appearing, and miracles blessing.

Right now, project your day or your tomorrow, or even your new year. Write an account of what you would like to take place using the power of divine visualization—as if it had already happened. You do not need to project everything because you can do this every day—pushing beyond the blindness of limitation to an unlimited vision of success. See with the vision that God has given you.

I decree blessings of the unseen here and now.

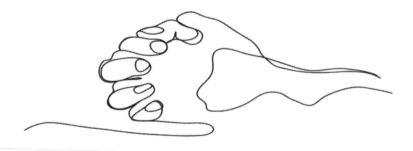

I Am Divine Intelligence

It's time to listen to the divine within.

On the fourth day, God said, let there be lights in the firmament of the heavens to divide the day from the night, and God made the two great lights, the greater light to rule the day, and the lesser light to rule the night (Genesis 1:14-16). The sun and the moon are the two great lights in the continuum of the creation story. Symbolically, these two great lights, the moon and the sun, are the *will* to accomplish our goals and the *understanding* that emerges to complete them. Our will and our understanding work in tandem.

The sun is the spiritual I AM, and the moon is the will. I am so grateful for this division of the "greater light" of the sun and the "lesser light" of the moon. I go to sleep willing—knowing the sun —the day—will provide guidance.

Unless it is a dire emergency, I have learned to let all projects sit overnight before finalizing them because I recognize this division between will and understanding in everything created. I allow myself to sit with ideas, sleep on them, let them simmer for a while. I love co-creating, trusting that with God's will moving through me, understanding will come. As opposed to our will, God's will is to participate fully in the creative flow.

In metaphysical symbology, the feet represent understanding, and the shoes represent the intellectual concepts that bind the mind in fixed attitudes or beliefs. When we are willing, we "remove our shoes" and become centered in the light within, which is understanding. We do not have to be conscious of these two energies working together but know that when Spirit guides us, they will.

Anger has a purpose, but when we fail to access compassion and all aspects of understanding that guide our will, there is chaos and destruction. Some understand that the pandemic's energy is the universe's creative power, keeping the ecosystem balanced.

Regardless of the appearances, we can work with Divine Intelligence to embody the fullness of Spirit as the Will of the Moon and the Understanding or Guidance of the Sun. In the morning, I always rise in that Divine Intelligence—stepping into the unknown, I witness the co-creative process each day.

If we try to solve a problem at the level of the problem, we are moving by sheer will. When we are lifted in divine understanding, we can operate beyond the confines of what appears to be a problem with Divine Intelligence. We do not need to know-how.

Instead, we need to trust that the how will reveal itself when the time comes.

I decree that I will do what understanding requires.

I See Through Now

It's time to embrace the now.

I stand in awe today—of life, of how important every breath is—of how magnificent it is to be given the opportunity to pour our souls into each measure of our existence and be as excited, enthusiastic, and energized as we possibly can be. We have experienced a cataclysm of disease, death, destruction, and despair, but rather than feel defeated, we have seized life by the horn. We have faced challenges and defied their ability to knock us to the ground. We have worked steadily, consistently, and courageously to center in a new boldness, a new energy, a new purpose, a new direction, a new focus that ensures we will emerge better.

I am reminded of Jacob wrestling with the angel in the 32nd book of Genesis. The Bible says that Jacob fought, that he struggled with an angel all through the night. It says that he told the angel, I am not going to let you go until you bless me (Genesis 32:26). Perhaps we used to think of our nights and days negatively but working and living remotely with social distancing gives us ample time to acknowledge their blessings. Jacob saw the blessing in his struggle with the angel, and he acknowledged its absolute good when he decided to keep fighting until he was blessed. The Bible says that the angel blessed Jacob saying, you are blessed because you have struggled with God and won (Genesis 32:28). He was blessed because he fought the good fight with the unseen and kept the faith. He awakened to see beyond what Jesus called the appearances of things. He awakened to see with a new faith.

Job had a lot of appearances to see beyond: he had lost family, property, and health. He was at ground zero with nothing left but a belief in God. He had to see absolute good to know that there was success beyond the appearances of things. Job 35:5 says, "Look to the heavens and see; and behold the clouds. They are higher than you."

Our law of seeing not only gives us the capacity to see beyond physical struggles and material pleasures but to look to a universe that is unlimited and absolute with good. It provides us with the ability to witness, know, shape, and form our future even before it manifests. Since this is a new portal of infinite opportunity that we are going through, we want to engage our ability to envision what is on the other side.

What is it that you see for yourself?

God has given us a canvas that we tend to waste. We tend to leave it blank, or even worse, we populate it with the negativity of news and the forecast of disaster because we are so steeped in the energy of an industry that profits from our fear, worry and stress. But how are you using your co-creative power to imagine a better world? If you could see anything as you emerge from this portal, what would it be? How would you like your life to change for the better? What would you like to offer, to be, to demonstrate? Your Father is an infinite world of unlimited good. Your Mother is a quantum realm of pure potential. What do you draw to yourself?

As Paul says (2 Corinthians 4:17-18), "do not look at the things which are seen, but at the things which are not seen. For the things which are seen are temporary, but the things which are not seen are eternal." See yourselves in the true light, as instruments of love—as beings of power. Allow the scales to fall from your eyes and witness absolute good in your souls.

We have wrestled with Jacob's angel, and by so doing, we have beat misery, lack, self-pity, addiction, suffering, lies, and sickness—and now we awaken. As always, we have an opportunity to create a new experience for ourselves.

Take a moment, and see with the spiritual eye, knowing that what you desire will manifest. Take a moment, open the vision boards of your souls, and allow God's good to pour into you, energize you, enlighten you, uplift you, paint you with miracles, joy, and grace. How do you see yourselves? How can you bless your past, present, and future to be receptive to endless opportunities? See with the power and the truth of the quantum realm, the spiritual energy of which we are all made. See the light of

Spirit handing you a brush that is ageless, timeless, formless, shapeless, and pouring into you a new faith to paint a new existence.

I decree endless opportunities.

I am Centered

It's time to center in God's good.

H ere is how we solidify our blessings. Here is how we renew the oneness of our connection with Spirit. As we move through these days of spiritual revitalization, we will align with the absolute good of the universe through the power of centering. If you center in the power of God, you will be changed. Centering in Spirit moves us beyond fear, worry, stress, shame, and hopelessness to realize our connection with all that Spirit is.

We must practice centering daily. We call it a practice because it is a spiritual muscle that we build. The best way to build your spiritual muscles is to be still, as the Psalmist says, and know that you are God (Psalm 46:10). It is a practice because sometimes, we are going to get it wrong. We may fail to practice, but we can always catch up by centering.

Centering is the silent practice of going within with appreciation of Spirit breathing through us. Centering in Spirit is purposefully aligning ourselves with God. Romans 3:19 says, "every mouth may be silenced and the whole world held accountable to God." In silence, we are accountable to God, and we can show up every day in accountability. We can stop talking and start listening.

In Luke 6:12, it says that "[n]ow it came to pass in those days that He went out to the mountain to pray and continued all night in prayer to God." The process of centering in God always manifests the miracles we need to move on in our lives and not be circumvented by temptation. All we need is a few minutes. Some say meditate for an hour, and if you do *not* have time, meditate for two hours. But all you need is 5-10 minutes to center.

Centering is our daily bread. We take the time to eat our daily bread, our manna, the spiritual food that God gives us each day by centering. No matter what happens in our lives, no matter what storms or discord occurs, centering gives us the peace, focus, and power that we need. Think of the daily bread as the morning meditation and the blood, the living water, as the evening silence.

In Mark 4:35-41, we learn that when a great windstorm arose, Jesus was in the stern, asleep on a pillow. The disciples awoke Him and said, "Teacher, do You not care that we are perishing?" Jesus arose, rebuked the wind, and said to the sea, "Peace, be still!" And the wind ceased, and there was a great calm. But He said to them, "Why are you so fearful? How is it that you have no faith?" In fear, they said to one another, "Who can this be, that even the wind and the sea obey Him!" Sometimes we feel like everything we do is like a windstorm, but we must center in the stillness during the storm.

I have been providing daily meditations for free for eight years at https://mindfulnessgroup.blog/ But here is a quick form of meditation to practice each day for a few minutes or more:

Close your eyes. Connect with the breath. Try to sit up straight, so you do not fall asleep. Feel your oneness with Spirit. Just breathe in and out your connection with Spirit. **Go to the altar of your soul but ask for nothing.**

Feel the lightness of air, breathing in and as you—until you are no longer separate. Feel the oneness with the breath. Allow your worries, concerns, cares, and reactions to disappear.

This impenetrable, omnipotent, omniscient, omnipresent force is known as God to many, Spirit to prophets, Source to believers, Vibration to others, Truth to students, Father to Jesus, Love to John. Be free, part of the unlimited freedom of God, one with the unlimited Truth of Spirit.

Find yourself centered in the heart of God. Realize the center of God is everywhere present. In this center, you are a magnet of the universe, attracting everything and everyone that you need in perfect divine order. In this center, you do not have to look for anything. Everything that you need is here. In this center, you are whole and complete. In this center, you are in harmony with those who support your greatest good, focused with love, directed through love, lifted as love.

In the center, there is no challenge, no obstacle that cannot be conquered. In the center, we are free from all sins. We are forgiven of all debts. We walk in the newness of life. In the center, your soul is washed; your mind is cleansed; your body is healed. Destiny opens new doors in the center, plants new seeds, and harvests new success without limits.

I decree that in the center, I am whole, prosperous and complete.

I am Guided by Spirit

It's time to have faith in Spirit.

Today, we are focused on the spiritual law of operation, how Spirit operates in our lives. Spirit is always operating in our lives for our greatest good. We do not have to worry about the things said or done against us because we realize that the universe conspires not to harm but to bless us.

We see how Spirit operates when we look at Hannah. Not only was Hannah barren, but she was married to a man who had another wife who was not barren. The other wife went out of her way to try to make Hannah's life a living hell. But even though the other wife appeared awful, she was part of God's operation because her nastiness is what led Hannah to prayer.

Hannah means grace. She stands for the transformative power of God in operation. She was miserable at first because she did not know how God operates. But Hannah eventually realized that she had to stop giving her energy to what she could not do alone and focus on what could be done through God. God operates in Spirit rather than in the flesh. When we give our energy to God, we experience the fullness of God's operations in all that we do. Often, we do not know the way; we do not have the resources; we lack power in the flesh, but we have to tap the power of God in operation, as the unlimited power that can do anything but fail.

When Hannah focused on the power of God in operation, she was no longer barren. She conceived and bore a son, the fruit of faith in what God can do. In 1 Samuel 1:20, the Bible says that she called him Samuel, saying, "Because I have asked the Lord for him." Samuel was the gift of God in operation. When we see and realize the presence of God, God will reveal so much more than the situation at hand. The Universe compels us to realize that the real lesson is giving birth in the Spirit to a faith that defies mere appearances. The law of operation teaches us that we do not have to worry about what we cannot do when we know what God can do.

Samuel means inner voice, spiritual discernment, ability to see beyond the material world. Hannah's faith in the operation of God was so powerful that when she gave birth to Samuel, spiritual discernment, she gave him to the temple to serve God. When we give our all to Spirit, the operation of God will bless us beyond what we could ever conceive in the flesh. 1 Samuel 2:21

says the Lord visited Hannah, so that she conceived and bore three sons and two daughters. Meanwhile, the child Samuel grew before the Lord. When Hannah stopped giving her thoughts and energy to the flesh and turned to the love and generosity of God in operation, she received more than she could ever imagine.

We also see how God operates in the story of Ruth. In Hebrew, Ruth means friend, but metaphysically, Ruth means love. Ruth's mother-in-law Naomi lost both her sons during a time of great famine. Naomi told her son's wives that they could go back to their families because she had nothing to offer them. Ruth stayed (Ruth 1:18-19). Naomi represents the soul. When love blesses the soul, the soul has all it needs.

Ruth worked in the fields. She reaped the bounty of the harvest. She fed Ruth, the soul, from her bounty. The operation of God led Ruth to work for Boaz, who was Naomi's wealthy relative. When he discovered what Ruth was doing for Naomi, he took care of them both. He gave Ruth enough food to share with Naomi, and he told his men to help Ruth in the fields.

God's operation blesses the infinite realm of generations to come. We are all part of a divine operation, which never stops giving birth to spiritual consciousness. This law teaches us that we are not limited, little or less but a magnificent expression of God's operation.

I decree God's operation at work in my life.

I Love Myself with Compassion

It's time to love ourselves.

In Colossians 3:12, Paul says that we must "clothe ourselves with compassion, kindness." Similarly, Matthew 14:14 says, "[w]hen Jesus landed and saw a large crowd, he had compassion on them and healed their sick." Before feeding the masses, Matthew 15:32 says Jesus called his disciples to him and said, "I have compassion for these people; they have already been with me three days and have nothing to eat." Matthew 20:34 says, "Jesus had compassion on [the blind] and touched their eyes. Immediately they received their sight and followed him."

Compassion opens our hearts to who we are, and through the acceptance of who we are, it focuses on us as the whole being of

God. As the whole being of God, we have the spaciousness and capacity to breathe with compassion in the moment and be fully present. We have the courage and strength to stare boldly into the face of our shame or regret. By facing it, we open our hearts to be better.

Shame is one of the most painful emotions that there is, causing deep trauma to the mind, body, and soul. Shame is so painful that it can spread through generations of those harmed, as well as through generations of the harmer. With shame, we hide our lights under bushels instead of shining the light that God gave us. Compassion is good medicine for shame. When we are compassionate, it does not mean that we reject our pain and suffering; compassion allows us to process it with a healing, restorative spirit. As the Nigerian poet Ijcoma Umebinyuo said, "[y]ou must let the pain visit. You must allow it to teach you." But she adds, "You must not allow it to overstay."

With compassion, we embrace our imperfections but also shift the narrative from drinking, abusing drugs, procrastinating, binging, comparing, harming ourselves, to liberation from our self-imposed shackles. We can pause and accept what is present and then be courageous enough to let it go.

I decree release of shame and pain.

I am the Even Greater Things

It's time to do even greater things.

I was listening to a story the other day about a young man who fought in the Vietnam War when he was 18 years old. He came face to face with a Vietnamese man, and he shot him, but after shooting him, he took a photo from his wallet of the Vietnamese man with a little girl. As time went on, he was increasingly horrified by what he had done. He began to look at the photo every day. Eventually, he wrote a letter to the man and asked for forgiveness, and he put it at the Vietnam Memorial. In the letter, he said, I will never know why you did not take my life; you stared at me so long, armed with your AK47, and yet you did not fire. Forgive me for taking your life. I was reacting the way I was trained. So often over the years, I stared at the picture of you and your daughter; each time, my heart would burn with the pain of guilt.

I have two daughters of my own now. I perceived you as a brave soldier defending his homeland. Above all else, I can respect the importance of what life held for you. I suspect that is why I am here today. It is time for me to continue the life process and release the pain and guilt. *Forgive me, sir.*

He eventually went to Vietnam in 2000 and somehow located the man's daughter, and he gave her the photo and told her it was the photo he took from her father's wallet on the day he killed him. He asked for her forgiveness.

After an awkward moment, she burst into tears and embraced him. Afterward, she told him that the day that he came to her and her brother, her father's spirit returned to them.

In Matthew 12:6, Jesus said, "something greater than the temple is here," and that greater something is the pure power and presence of God. *The greater things that we are here to do are taking advantage of the most difficult things in our lives and pushing beyond their edges as the most significant opportunities to shift the world around us, to step outside of our comfort zones, to test the edges of our capacity, to dig deep in the creative soil of our consciousness, to love greater than we could ever imagine, to make this world a better place.*

The greatest commandment provides the foundation for the greater things that we must do: love your neighbor as yourself. True greatness acts with humility. As Jesus teaches us in Luke 22:27, when he says, "[f]or who is greater, the one who is at the table or the one who serves? Is it not the one who is at the table? But I am among you as one who serves."

In John 5:20, Jesus says, "[f]or the Father loves the Son and shows him all he does. Yes, and he will show him even greater works than these so that you will be amazed." The greater things that God reveals to us are not limited but align with the consciousness of Christ and the guidance of the Holy Spirit.

The law of even greater things is captured in John 14:12, when Jesus said, "[v]ery truly I tell you, whoever believes in me will do the works I have been doing, and they will do even greater things than these, because I am going to the Father."

This means that we can do more than walk water, heal more than the lame, increase more than two fish and five loaves of bread, rise from our mats of affliction, cast more than the spirits of demons into the sea, be more than a single garment for one woman to touch and be made whole. We can do more than make the blind see, more than raise a man from the dead, more than be resurrected from the limitations of the material world.

In John 14:19-20, Jesus says, "[b]efore long, the world will not see me anymore, but you will see me. Because I live, you also will live. On that day, you will realize that I am in my Father, and you are in me, and I am in you." There is a greater power in us than is in the world. The only way that we will navigate obstacles, seize more than mere moments, move beyond mountains is to realize that we are not waiting on but are the pure power of God.

As children made in God's image and likeness, we are greater than the world. We, too, Jesus is teaching us are greater than the flesh. We are everyone, everything, everywhere, and yet no one, nothing, and no one because Christ is in us, and we are in Christ, and together we are the whole body of all that God is.

The law of even greater things says that we are here to use our power. Whatever there is that you desire to do, dream of doing something greater. If you want peace, be peaceful. If you want forgiveness, be forgiving. If you want harmony, be harmonious. If you want grace, be graceful. If you want to feed your baby, feed hungry children everywhere. If you want to support your family, support a change that will never allow anyone to suffer. If you want to lift yourself up by the grace of God, be a beacon of the living God and shine the light of your grace on others. If you want to heal your life, open your heart to heal the hearts of others.

And do not worry about the how—the details of what you shall eat, or what you shall drink, or wear—because the Father knows what you need before you even ask. But seek first the Kingdom of God. Be even greater than you can imagine. The possibilities to manifest are unlimited.

I decree that I am ready to do the greater things that I must do.

I am God's Image and Likeness

It's time to see God in our reflection.

I am a co-creative power of Spirit, with the ability to shape, mold, and co-create with infinite source. Newton's theory of life as mere shape, form, and matter was debunked by Einstein's famous equation $E = mc2$, demonstrating that energy and matter are the same. We shape energy with our minds, hearts, and souls because consciousness is energy. Thus, genes do not control our lives. Epigenetics teaches us that we can change our belief systems and rewrite the genetic expressions of our lives. We are not limited by race, class, or background; we are only limited by our perceptions.

Race is a construct. White people made up the idea of race to support the lie of superiority to oppress people of color and marginalize, denigrate, colonize, and control for profit. This construct permeates everything to such an extinct that many non-White people do not even like themselves. We all have the same potential. But because of the construct of race and class, we tend to get in our own way. We need to get out of the way.

In Genesis 1:26-27, God said, "[l]et us make man in our image, in our likeness, and let them rule over the fish of the sea and the birds of the air, over the livestock, over all the earth, and over all the creatures that move along the ground." So, God created man in His own image; in the image of God, he created him; male and female, he created them. We are all the pure energy of God, having a human experience. We are only limited by the restrictions, inhibitions, and doubts we place upon ourselves.

On the first day, the scripture teaches us that God said let there be light. Let there be light today. Let us be lifted in spiritual illumination. Let us realize that we are co-creative powers of Spirit. Let us open our minds, hearts, and souls to guide us when we need guidance, to reveal our divine purpose, to free us from self-imposed restrictions, to bless our bodies with unimaginable strength, to breathe the breath of a new awareness, to loosen the grip of old sins, to be reborn in triumph. I release what no longer serves me, and I embrace the co-creative power that I am.

I decree I am God's image and likeness.

I am the Light

It's time to shine our light.

Genesis means origin. We are all the beginning of the co-creative power of God, who is not an old white man in the sky. Creation did not begin in seven days and then stop but continues through us. The light of our beginning is our awareness of pure potential. Let there be light speaks not only to the fullness of God's power but also the illumination that we reflect as children of God. Let there be light, we say during this pandemic. Let us move forth with a new awareness to be guided through the unknown.

The illumination we seek, the knowledge of God, *is within us.* Expand your notion of the power and presence of God. Lean into a new awareness of Spirit as divine energy, all around you. Let there be light. Let here be a revelation. Let there be an epiphany. Let there be an opening in whenever we are stuck. As Jesus said,

"I am the light of the world," the "I Am." You "are the light of the world." So "let your light shine." "Let there be light" opens us to the full awareness of our ability to create whatever we need when we need it.

I decree acceptance of the light of the divine.

I am Divine Source

It's time to realize inexhaustible source.

On the second day, when God said, let there be a firmament amid the waters, God was talking about a foundation of the faith of absolute knowing: trust that stands underneath all things. Firmament means a firm, unwavering place in consciousness, a bit more than faith. Faith is belief, hope, longing for something we want to see take place. But firmament is the pure substance of absolute good. Firmament is not merely believing that our good will manifest but is its manifestation.

If what we see is energy and our thoughts are energy, we have the power to mold and shape and co-create this energy as the firmament, the substance, the divine source everywhere present. Regardless of what confronts us, what matters is how we choose to tell the story and co-create with Divine Source. Divine Source is not limited by form but is the energy of the kingdom that we cannot see. When we breathe in the moment and loosen our grip on the appearances around us, we become one with co-creative energy, the source of everything. We shift from being locked inside the body to becoming one with the consciousness of God, a canvas of infinite ideas.

Ideas are inexhaustible in the ethers of quantum realm's no place, nowhere, no time, nothing. Inexhaustible source blesses us without ceasing as we wield the power that molds and shapes it. As co-creator, become one with pure potential, with illumination and source – with every expectation of the unlimited divine and guided into the best experiences.

Divine Source is aligning synchronicities for your desired outcomes. Your good is coming from Infinite Source. Be gracious, loving and kind to everyone, so you do not block your good. Breathe in the awareness that the universe conspires to help us, and pure consciousness aligns our best outcome.

*I decree what I need
is manifesting for me.*

I Trust God

It's time to trust Absolute Good.

Genesis 2:2-3 says by the seventh day, God had finished the universe's work, so on the seventh day, God rested. Then God blessed the seventh day and made it holy. As we navigate the thousands of deaths and sickness of the pandemic, the police murders and other brutalities, and the jailing of children, we awaken from our slumber to realize the need to support one another, stop fighting, and embrace one another with compassion and peace.

The struggle is not us against them; it is us against injustice, against inequity, unfairness, marginalization, and denigration by anyone or anyone. Any attitude that does not welcome our fellow human beings is the fault of those whose failure to condemn wrongdoing supports its activity. God has a peculiar way of using us to energize, guide, direct, uproot, rectify, revolutionize, transform, change our hearts to make us love one another.

The seventh day does not mean doing nothing; it means trusting in God. Trust is the daily work that we continue to do despite the storm, the discipline that we have all shown each day, the accountability of our souls to do the work, the meditation practice that we must maintain, the surrender to the Spirit of the Lord to proclaim that God is a great God that never fails. God fills our hearts, minds, and souls with the direction we must take, the ideas that we must accomplish.

Some will be on the front lines of protest because that is their calling. You have to discern your own. We must trust to the point of knowing that a better day will not just come; beneath the chaos, it is already here. What, beloved, will you do with it?

I decree that we will win the fight for equity.

Do Not Be Afraid

It's time to stop being afraid.

In Exodus 14:13, Moses said, "do not be afraid, stand firm, and you will see the deliverance the Lord will bring you today." Lift yourselves out of the realm of fear to stand not apart but as one with God, to radiate the perfect love that is your birthright as a child of Spirit. We call out to God as though God is separate from who we are, but the scripture teaches us that we are the whole being of Spirit expressing as us. Stand strong in the perfect peace of who you are today—more Spirit than flesh. Stand strong in resilience today. Stand strong in perfect health and wholeness today. Stand strong in miracles today. Stand strong in victory today. Stand strong in favor today. Stand strong in everything you need to realize what you need whenever you need it.

The Deuteronomist says, "do not be afraid of them. The Lord your God himself will fight for you" (3:22). Moses says in Exodus 20:20, "do not be afraid, God has come to test you so that the fear of God will be with you to keep you from sinning." Doubt is sin. Worry is sin. Despair is sin. To the test of whatever falls before us, John 8:44 speaks to it, saying, "for there is no truth in him, when he lies, he speaks his native language, for he is a liar and the father of lies." Do not be afraid, Moses said, because your test reveals your triumph, and the cup that looks half empty really is half full.

As children of God, we are stronger than our prayers. We send this healing energy throughout our communities, homes, work-places, and other spaces worldwide. We pour this energy of love, of perfect health and wholeness to everyone, this energy that will wipe out any virus, this energy that will keep our children safe, that will protect our elders, our communities, our loved ones, and each one of us. As Jesus said in John 14:27, my peace I leave with you, my peace I give you. Accept this peace today. Wash your souls in it. Be at peace that every plague will pass. Receive God's good in peace. Let it bless your rooms, heal your body, and bring us closer together with the victory of whatever ails us, departing just as quickly as it comes.

I decree I am the courage of Spirit.

We are More Spirit Than Flesh

It's time to realize we are more Spirit.

I looked up the definition of pandemic. It means a widespread outbreak of disease. Through the appearances of disease, we are all impacted physically, but in Spirit, we transcend the problems of the physical world. Since we are more Spirit than flesh, we can connect with the wholeness of all that is, an energy of perfect health. We call those things that appear to defy physical time, place, or order—miracles. But they are really the greater things that Spirit does through us.

The scripture says, physician, heal thyself; get up off your mat and walk. We are all healers, if we choose to work with the power that resides within us and within which we reside. We change our biology during meditation and prayer, not because something in the external operates on us but because we embrace the kingdom of God within us. In the kingdom, there is no sickness, no dis-ease, no pandemic. When asked where the kingdom was, Jesus said it is neither left nor right—here nor there: the kingdom of God is within us. We are temples of a living God.

Here and now, we tap the incredible powers that we have and bless all of those around us. We send our love of peace and protection to everyone in the world. In the same way that disease spreads, so can healing, so can perfect health and wholeness. We have the power to bring about change rather than merely react to what is going on around us. But we must lift ourselves up in higher consciousness and be accountable for sharing love, light, energy, and joy.

Every step we take, every thought we think should remind us that we are also pure beings of Spirit, having a human experience. We are not here to neglect but give the pure energy of grace to bless, protect, and send that healing energy, light, and awareness to all around us. Let us see millions being made whole and the appearance of disease disappearing. Let us see people getting up from their mats well, with new strength and awareness of their own healing power.

I decree perfect health and wholeness.

We are in the Father, and Jesus is in Us, and We are in Him

It's time to know that we are one.

W hen we come together and share a like mind of strength, courage, and compassion, we operate from a consciousness steeped in John 14:20 when Jesus says, "I am in the Father, and you are in me, and I am in you." There is no separation between us and our highest good. We are the wholeness, we are the absolute good, we are the image and likeness of perfect health that we seek. Let us be lifted in this divine energy and not be enslaved to the news. We only need to stay informed but not give the media our power. We can choose when to unplug from the nonstop negative, which only lowers our vibrations.

In God, there is no disease, no virus, no sickness. In God, there is absolute good. Just take a moment and feel the love of God radiating through you. Send that vibration of love and light to everyone in our communities. Send it throughout our workplaces, churches, parks, city agencies, and nursing homes. Tear down the barriers that have divided us in the past: barriers of race, language, politics, religion, sexual preference, national origin, and other differences.

We can feel our heart centers of love and start with healing ourselves. Rub your hands together and feel the energy of power illuminating from you. Extend your hands outward to spread love to others. Resonate in love, knowing that you are continuously regenerating brand-new cells in your body without any guidance. Throughout the day, we can recenter ourselves in this awareness that we are one with the Spirit. As Jesus said in John 14:20, I am in the Father, and you are in me, and I am in you. We send this divine connection of love to everyone, everywhere, regardless of race, creed, culture, age, sexual expression, or national origin, and we see our planet in perfect health and wholeness.

I decree that I am the whole being of all that Spirit is.

We Are a Vibration of Victory

It's time to applaud our victories.

Let us breathe in calm and breathe out peace. Let us breathe in joy and breathe out wholeness. Let us breathe in love and breathe out gratitude. Breathe in light and breathe out victory. Breathe in wisdom and breathe out truth. Breathe in now and breathe out forever. And in each breath that we take, let us be aware that we are whole. We are the good that penetrates everyone everywhere, and no one nowhere. We can breathe the light of wholeness from the past, not only observing every cell, every molecule, every vessel, every organ but filling it with strength, filling it with wisdom, filling it with gratitude and the regenerative power of absolute good. We can breathe in the perfect peace of now; and allow it to bless every crack, crevice, and space with success, with divine knowledge, triumph, truth-telling and uplifting, and giving everybody exactly what they need when they need it.

Let us celebrate the now as nothing more or less than the breath of simply being, which we tend to take for granted. We can breathe in forgiveness, release, and surrender, letting go, cleansing, healing. We can breathe in the truth of the future and allow victory to flow through our veins: a victory of health, a victory of compassion, a victory of synergy, a victory of transformation, a victory of rebirth, a victory of overcoming, a victory of knowing.

We can walk the water of a new faith, asking and receiving, seeking and finding, knocking and realizing the door is open. We can appreciate each moment, glance, step, word, chance, breath, now for all that it is, in all that we are. Everything within and without is always emitting light; even when we live in survival mode under the burden of stress, we draw from this invisible field of energy, and our light is enhanced. More light is emitted from our bodies, minds, and souls, less matter, and more vital energy.

There is a future in us that already exists in the present moment. When asked in Luke 17:21 where the Kingdom of God is, Jesus says it is neither here nor there; the Kingdom of God is within you.

In John 8:12, Jesus said I am the light of the world. He said whoever follows me will never walk in darkness—but will have the light of life. This was the same light that God saw as good when the world was created, a light that is separate from darkness as in Genesis 1:4. This was the same light that God gave the Israelites, who represent thought striving for higher consciousness as they were liberated from Egypt (worldly consciousness), a guiding light that illuminated their path to travel by day or night (Exodus 13:21). This is the same light the Psalmist sang about when he said the Lord is my light and salvation. Whom shall I fear?

In Spirit's light, we see the light. In Matthew 5:14, Jesus says, you are the light of the world: a town built on a hill cannot be hidden. First John teaches us this light is all that God is: a light that penetrates all darkness. In John 12:36, Jesus said believe in the light so that you may become children of light. First Peter 29 says you are a chosen people, a Royal priesthood, a holy nation, God's special possession that you may declare the praises of him who called you out of darkness into his marvelous light.

Today, we redeem ourselves in light. We are saved in light. We are anointed in light. We are resurrected in light. The miracles that pour from our souls are the light. See that man lifted from his mat at Bethesda, or that woman cured from her issue of blood, or the blind that can now see, or the virus that has disappeared, or the miraculous healings that have taken shape, or the disappearance of what we thought was a struggle—those challenges lifted us out of our darkness so that we can now see we are illuminated by the light that is everywhere present.

*I decree that in the Kingdom of Absolute Good,
there is only the light of loving grace.*

Lead Beyond the Edge of Now

It's time to get out of our way.

Leading beyond the edge of now requires us to get out of our own way, believe beyond appearances, rise with the power within, and leave our comfort zone where we indulge in the fantasy of can't but know deep in our hearts that we can. Belief is power. Seeing beyond the physical into the unlimited realm of absolute good is power. Realizing in the depths of our inner most being that we are the pure potential of a God that has no boundaries—is without parameters, or definition, or limitation is power. Some people have made billions off the economy—who shifted their investments so that they could take advantage of our lowest experience. How can we co-create a world that flourishes in plenty during the appearances of lack?

Leading beyond the edge of now is an opportune time to grow beyond the fear and the frustration of what we see in the flesh to the fantastic ability to be fulfilled in the Spirit. What if Jesus never stepped beyond the edge of what he saw in the flesh—water never would have turned to wine, the blind never would have seen, fish and bread never would have multiplied. Leading beyond the edge is the crossroads at which we choose Spirit over the physical, Spirit over turmoil, Spirit over loss, Spirit over division, Spirit over now with each step we take.

When Jesus was just 12 years old, and his parents were looking for him. They found him three days later, sitting in a temple in Jerusalem. The Bible says that he was surrounded by Jewish scholars, rabbis who had studied the word of God. The scripture says that the learned men were asking this 12-year old questions, and they were astounded by his wisdom. But the part of this scripture that always resonated with me is in Luke 2:48-29 when Jesus' parents tell him, "Son, we were looking everywhere. We were worried to death." Jesus said, "there's no need for you to worry about me because you see, I am always about My Father's business."

My Father's business requires me to lead beyond the edge of what you expect of me in the now and step into the courage of what I am called to do—studying and growing beyond the parameters of what you think. I cannot limit myself to what you think. I move beyond the mediocre, beyond the ordinary, beyond the status quo.

Leading beyond the edge of now requires me to move with the Spirit. Lifted in the power of our Father's business, we can step out into the vast realm of unknowing, realizing that we are guided by Spirit, blessed by Spirit, prospered by Spirit, pushed outside of our boxes by Spirit—to become wiser, deeper, stronger.

Nothing in the flesh can limit us. We can cut the core of our own limitations and fly. This is not about what you can do beloved, it is about what God does through you. When we are doing what we are called to, God will provide the answers. The people that we need will show up. The resources that are always available will reveal themselves. The only thing that we should do is get out of our way and trust God to do the rest.

Bless your challenges! Bless what seems problematic. A Unity teacher Mary Alice always said, call it all good; call it all joy. Everything that is part of our enjoyment will begin the mysterious process of transforming water into wine—doubt into determination, misery into the miraculous, frustration into the fantastic. Each step is a process that we can grow through with joy. 2 Peter 3:18 says grow in the grace and knowledge of Christ.

Leading beyond the edge of now is the realization that God gives us what we need— to do what we were called to do. We are growing into the full expression of God's creation. We can paint on the canvas of new life—with brushes of dreams and textures of possibility. We can stretch beyond the unknown—bold enough to plant the right seeds, to start with a new script, to move so far beyond what used to contain us that our boxes become a vague memory that we have stepped out of—so that when we look back, we are not stuck in fear but are a catalyst for change.

I decree that we are more than limitations.

Sing Soul Praises of Divine Purpose

It's time to sing through the power of our soul.

They say that there was a secret chord that David played that pleased the Lord. You see, when he was a shepherd boy, he was often summoned to play on his harp for King Saul. If you read the psalms, you see in Psalm 146, David says while "I live will I praise the Lord; I will sing praises to my God while I have any being." David established the importance of connecting with our own rhythm, our own gifts and talents, our own beat to bring light and full fruition to the power that Spirit radiates as us to the world.

How many of us are sitting on our full potential, stopping short of our tremendous capacity and purpose to be used by the universe? I was listening to Ram Dass, who said that this life experience is fourth grade, a grade school plane of experience to get it right and develop consciousness. I believe it is more than that: this life experience is to do what the daffodils, the lilies, and the oak trees do. We are here to be the most awesome self we can be, like the birds and the whales and the peacock—to be a full expression of our magnificence.

COVID-19 has not summoned us to a halt; it has catapulted us beyond convention to tap our purest potential to be our best, shine our lights, and rise in the fullness of the infinite possibilities of what we are here to do. If you are holding back, hiding the ball, succumbing to lethargy or laziness, you have failed to shine the light of your full capacity—taking from others and giving nothing of yourself. You have failed to sing your praise song to God.

Are you singing, or are you mumbling or just mouthing the words to your song? We need to sing our own song—and let it be heard loud and clear over the rooftops of our inhibitions, down past the barriers of our self-consciousness, between the blocks that we placed in front of all that we are and all that we can be.

We need to sing our song, and let it be a jazz beat with a gospel rhythm, a hip-hop rap between a rock and roll clap, a stone-cold blues note that has the potential to save souls all in one breath. We need to sing our song, dance our dance, speak our speech, take our stand, run our race, and paint our picture because that's what we are here for—that's what we were called to do.

Jesus said we are the light of the world. Nobody should light a lamp and put it under a bowl. He says, put your lamp on its stand

and give light to everyone in the house. Stop worrying about what other people think. Stop putting yourselves inside of the straight-jacket of other people's opinions. Stop limiting yourself to what you see in the world and enlarge your territory to the unlimited vortex you know in your soul. God is calling each of us to be fresh, original, and free. In *Song of Myself*, Walt Whitman says, "I celebrate myself and sing myself." Whitman says, "I know that the hand of God is the promise of my own."

Competition is based on the error thoughts that God's good is limited. We believe that there is only one prize, a limited supply of good. But the universe is filled with an abundance of everything for everyone. We want to walk between the lines and recite somebody else's poem and sing someone else's song because we are afraid of being *too much*. But being *too much* or extraordinary or different is a great thing.

While I live, I will praise the Lord with the unlimited creative capacity of all that I am, vibrant, remarkable, colorful, astounding, authentic, beautiful, amazing, loving, enlightened, talented, strong, powerful, present, centered—flowing with the infinite stream of energy known as me—and God in Christ and me and glory in me and hope in me. I'm going to sing the song of words through me, speech through me, movement through me, leadership through me, Spirit through me, divine ideas through me. Sing your song, no matter how out of synch it seems. Sing your song, and let it be a loud and clear expression of all that you are and all that you can be. Sing your song and let it be your cadence and your passion and your poetry and your dance and your deliverance.

Allow the Spirit of God's eternal voice to sing through you. Allow the infinite rhythms of the universe to ignite your soul into the divine mind of the blessings that are just waiting to unfold from you—just simply being you. Today is the day that we rise in the grace of our being and celebrate the movement, the magic, the miracle that we are in the infinite potential of every wave of the quantum realm flowing through our existence of nothing, no one, and nowhere but the fullness and the presence of Spirit.

When we sing who we are to the full capacity of our voices, our skills, and our gifts to be here and now singing absolute good to the world, we co-create Spirit's most beautiful ideas. This is our now. This is our truth. This is our time to use each minute wisely.

I decree a song of the unlimited capacity of all that God is.

We are the Balm in Gilead

It's time to heal with a balm of wholeness.

This is in many respects a time of war, a war among principalities of the unseen, a war for change whose time we have long-awaited, a war that requires us to win as it is a turning point in the lives that we lead and the space that we take up. Jeremiah 8:22 raises the question, "Is there no balm in Gilead, Is there no physician there?" Gilead is the mountain where Jacob fled when he needed to find a safe space from his father-in-law, who held Jacob captive, and it was there that Jacob was liberated through a covenant (Genesis 31:21). Metaphysically, Gilead is a place of transformation, of strength bearing witness to change. Gilead is the high place in consciousness where Spirit discerns truth for our own medicine's healing power. Where is the balm of Gilead? The balm is the Spirit.

Spirit is everywhere present, universal intelligence that goes before us, inexhaustible supply that opens endless channels of blessings. Spirit is the guidance of our counselor, our teacher, and our guide. The ability to forgive, let go of anchors of fear, resentment, shame, blame, and liberate ourselves in the pure love of Spirit is good medicine.

Good medicine is the ability to heal by realizing that no past-present-future-time-space-body-limitation has power over us, but we are the power of perfect health and wholeness, power beyond a doubt, power to exhale with the presence of a Father-Mother-God that we know as the air that we breathe and space that we take up. The ability to honor the image and likeness we were made with wisdom, presence, and power is good medicine.

Let us drink good medicine fully in our souls today. Let us uplift it in our words, dress our wounds in it, wear it in every garment, and use it to wash every limb, bone, and organ of truth and know that good medicine answers our call before we even ask.

I decree that I will take good medicine.

We Shall All
Be Changed

It's time to change.

I was up this morning, at the crack of dawn, digging
deeper for the good medicine of peace, when I came
across a great lesson by African American writer, Buddhist, and genius award winner Charles R. Johnson in his book
Taming the Ox. Johnson says if we can "remember that politics is
merely the skin of social life beneath which we find a more profound experience of ourselves and others, then our
Constitution-mandated sea change every four years can potentially be an uplifting experience rather than a spiritually
debilitating one. For as the Buddhist nun Jingnuo wrote four
centuries ago, 'If you bring to everything an illumined mind, you

won't get lost.'" Bringing an illumined mind requires us to realize that the physical is only a part of who we are.

Do not pray, Eric Butterworth taught, to God, but pray from the consciousness of God. Declare for yourself: "I am a spiritual being with the potential for peace and harmony and overcoming within me at all times. I am a radiating center of divine light, life, and wisdom." Then, you take your place in the world as bringers of light rather than as purveyors of darkness. We can declare that we are children of God, radiating light, love, and peace. We can be the new day instead of the old error ways, a new person who realizes there is strength in compassion, the awakening of Spirit in tune with the positive flow of divine life.

True change is not in the physical alone but with the understanding that good medicine is the power of the kingdom that dwells in us and in which we dwell. We can smooth on the good medicine of recognizing our oneness with the divine, our connection with the creator, our transformation as peacemakers who speak the word and make it so. Good medicine reminds us that we wear the truth and walk in the wisdom of a new day, that no weapon formed against us shall prosper. In good medicine, we realize our wounds can be healed in a simple amen, which is not an ending but an acceptance that all we seek is done.

I decree that we are the power and peace of good medicine.

Stop Limiting Yourselves to Re-Runs of the Past

It's time to release the past.

We have the power to liberate ourselves from experiencing the same things over and over again by our ability to stop thinking the same thoughts. We can free ourselves from the past by no longer being trapped in the old way of thinking. We can be transformed by the renewal of our minds and the true baptism of the Spirit.

Matthew 3:1-3 teaches us about our ability to repent. Repenting is releasing the past to be accountable for the present. The ancient text says, "In those days came John the Baptist, preaching in the wilderness of Judaea, and saying, 'Repent all of you: for the kingdom of heaven is at hand. For this is he that was spoken of by the prophet Isaiah, saying, 'The voice of one crying in the wilderness,' Prepare all of you the way of the Lord, make his paths straight.'"

The words of John the Baptist reveal to us that we can be renewed in the Spirit. We are not locked into our current circumstances, but we can always be made new. Repent, John said, for the Kingdom of Heaven is at hand. Repent means to shift our perspective, to change our minds, to exercise our free will to be dissatisfied with who we are and what the world looks like so that we can be made new, so that we can unlock potential, so that we can experience and be better than we have ever realized.

Paul says I die daily. I stop doing what I did yesterday. I stop living in the re-runs of who I have been so that I can be what I am. I stop giving my power to other people and take responsibility for who I am. I stop giving my energy to the same routine as yesterday, allowing my tomorrow to be a lot like my yesterday, letting my yesterday create my tomorrow.

My power is my ability to change my life instantly, snap my consciousness into a new wave of thought, and be the whole being of the universe, expressing as me in a new way, changing old vibrations to accept the unlimited greatness of who I am. This shift allows me to change the expression of what I once thought was hard-wired. I can alter the biology, genetic composition of my ancestors and liberate myself from their trauma. This means I can change my immune system, halt genes activated for inflammation and disease, and turn on new genes for growth and repair. But I am what I believe, so I first accept the greater power of Spirit expressing as me.

In Spirit, I am unlimited. As the image and likeness of all that is, I can change my body. I can co-create new genes, make new healthy proteins, strengthen my internal defense system. I can reduce the stress that is depleting the power of Spirit expressing as me and instead tap into and turn on my receptivity to the wholeness of God.

I will die daily, liberating my body and mind and my tendency to allow the past to sit in my presence, judging and condemning and shaming who I am now. The truth is that I am free. In each breath, I am whole and well. I have the freedom to be nobody in each second, thus wiping the slate empty and starting anew again. *As nobody, no one, nowhere, and nothing, I am fully liberated in the consciousness of Christ to start again, to express the miracle of simply being one with God. In God, I am the pure energy of love and light. I stop being satisfied with less than, and I open my heart to accepting my full potential as a child of God. I release the roles that I used to play, and I breathe in the expression of my highest self without fear, reluctance, or my inner critic, limiting thoughts.*

Repenting means denying the power of anything other than love over us, releasing, letting go, forgiving, and simply listening to God, trusting the Holy Spirit, and making ourselves fully available to our teacher, our counselor, and our guide. Repentance is not about shame, blame, or guilt but about moving out of our way so that we can embody the fullness of God.

I repent, but not as a sinner. I repent affirming the fullness of Spirit as my good, perfect health and wholeness, my manifestation of all of those things that I desire before they have even taken shape. I repent in the full understanding of our ability to shape, our ability to transform, our ability to heal, our ability to ask and receive.

I decree that I can let go and let God.

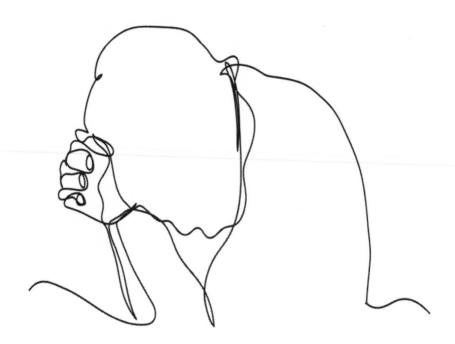

We Are in a Planetary Evolution

It's time to appreciate our evolution.

I am energized by this moment, lifted in the highest realm of all that Spirit is. I am blessed by the absolute good of light that shines in me and is everywhere present. In this breath, I breathe a virus of faith, a contagion of grace, and an outpouring of love. I bless every soul with a gift of service for the good of all.

Today, we can break our ties to the old and summon the new. We don't need to repair what we can co-create. Yes, there is cause and effect, but the quantum realm, unlimited source, blesses us with grace. In grace, we are brand new. Don't try to put your old life back together. Be busy co-creating the new you. Keep finding the present moment and creating from the nothingness of absolute good. Some call that a miracle, but it is a new beginning that is always available to us.

The true miracle is our acceptance of the power that is our birthright. In the sanctuary of our homes, we go away for a while and process the present moment. But this moment is not limiting; it is liberating because, as students of Spirit, we can open ourselves up to a new awareness that we have the power to impact change through higher consciousness. The quantum realm allows us to empty our minds of material limitations to more fully embrace spiritual power.

In Romans 8:9, Paul teaches us that we are not controlled by sin but by the Spirit if we accept the presence of the Spirit of God that lives in us. 1 Corinthians 3:16 asks us whether we know ourselves as God's temple? God's Spirit lives in us. As Paul says in Acts 17:28: "for in Him, we live and move and have our being." In this consciousness, the healing that needs to take is waiting to bless us with absolute good.

I decree that we are the evolution of Spirit.

Raise the Power of Your Greatness

It's time to uplift the power of greatness.

I am focused on the power of pride today. The truth is that we often fail to celebrate who we are, what we have come through, what we have overcome, what makes us magnificent. We fail to love ourselves. Many now realize that bodies racialized as black have been marginalized, denigrated, and condemned as less than. But we also need to address our power, our strength, and our excellence. What can we do to raise the banner of our greatness? Can we move forward in step with appreciation of who we are and where we have come from? Can we stop limiting ourselves to someone else's definition of who we are and stare deeply into the face of our own love?

The late John Lewis took pride in himself. He was the son of sharecroppers and an apostle of nonviolence bloodied at Selma and across the Jim Crow South in the historic struggle for racial equality. "I have been in some kind of fight—for freedom, equality, basic human rights—for nearly my entire life," he said. Galatians 6:4 says, "Each one should test their own actions. Then they can take pride in themselves alone, without comparing themselves to someone else."

Take pride in the love of God breathing through your excellence. Take pride in your march, your step, your gait, your ability, your triumph, your victory, your truth.

Pride is often undermined as negative, especially when people use it to attempt to marginalize others. But that is false pride. Genuine pride is the positive praise in our abilities to be greater than we have ever imagined and to take inventory of our victories, so that we can shine our lights for all to see. God takes pride in expressing as each one of us, but we must also take pride in God radiating as our greatness.

In *God is a Brown Girl Too*, God says, "when you know that I am you and you are me, you will begin to discover who God is." God is love, and we reconnect with the energy of God's love through the breath, and so we breathe mindfully. Right here and right now, breathe in and re-discover your divine connection with God; remember that God is breathing you as the greatest gift of love that there is. Close your eyes and breathe, realizing that you awaken to your power with each breath you take. In each breath that you take, you know that you have nothing to fear.

Philippians 3:6 tells us how much God loves us. God says, do not be anxious about anything; just give your requests to me.

Take pride in your divine connection with infinite source. Move beyond the sound where your voice asks God and go to the space where your soul listens. God is always talking to us if we would just listen. *Take a second right now and listen.* Isaiah told you that "[w]hen you turn to the right or when you turn to the left, your ears shall hear a word behind you saying, 'This is the way, walk in it'" (Isaiah 30:21). When we really listen, we can hear the Universe, saying "I love you – with an everlasting love."

Take pride in your divine vision. See the love that surrounds you with an aura of loving energy, and fills your body temple with wholeness, and goes before you as all-powerful love to do the work that you were appointed to do, to march, to appoint, to deliver, to contribute your light and uplift your greatness in the same way that John Lewis did. *He showed us that when we stand together with pride in who we are and our ability to move forward as a people, nothing is impossible.*

As Lewis said, "[i]t was very moving, very moving to see hundreds of thousands of people from all over America and around the world take to the streets—to speak up, to speak out, to get into what I call 'good trouble,'" about the recent protests, he said there is no turning back.

The Universe has already aligned to give us what we want, manifest the answers that we need, and bless us with the gifts that await us. Let us take pride in stretching beyond where we are to be even better: stretch beyond hate into love, stretch beyond fear into love, stretch beyond jealousy into love. Stretch beyond resistance, tightness, and anxiety with love. Just allow yourselves to stretch beyond whatever box you are in with the love that pushes even beyond pride to give its best without the need for recognition or reward.

I decree that I stretch beyond limits with pride.

• DAY 33 •

Whatever We Believe, We Will Receive

It's time to believe.

In Matthew 21, we learn that early one morning, when Jesus was on his way back to the City of Bethany, he saw a fig tree by the road, and because he was hungry, he searched its branches but found nothing but leaves. Then Jesus said to it, "[m]ay you never bear fruit again." When his disciples saw this, they were amazed and asked him how the fig tree died so quickly? Jesus said, "I tell you the truth, if you have faith and do not doubt, not only can you do what was done to the fig tree, but also say to this mountain, 'go throw yourself into the sea,' and it will be done. He said, "If you believe, you will receive whatever you ask for in prayer."

In Luke 11, Jesus says, "[s]uppose one of you has a friend, and he goes to him at midnight and says, 'Friend, lend me three loaves of bread, because a friend of mine on a journey has come to me, and I have nothing to set before him.' Then the one inside answers, 'Don't bother me. The door is already locked, and my children are with me in bed. I can't get up and give you anything.' I tell you, though he will not get up and give him the bread because he is his friend, yet because of the man's boldness, he will get up and give him as much as he needs." When we believe that we will receive what we ask for, we receive it. We are only limited by our consciousness. Jesus says, "[a]sk and it will be given to you; seek and you will find; knock and the door will be opened to you. For everyone who asks receives; he who seeks finds; and to him who knocks, the door will be opened."

The open door of our consciousness is vibrational coherence, when what we know and believe is in complete harmony with what we think and feel and resonates with every aspect of who we are. When our vibrations align with Spirit, we manifest what we ask for quicker because we believe that we will receive it.

We vibrate your truth from our whole being. Our words and actions on the outside need to be backed up by our vibration on the inside. Our desire is not something we labor to fulfill but the recognition of something we already possess: assuming the feeling of being that we desire to be so that believing and being are one.

Truth depends upon the intensity of our imagination, not upon external facts. We become what we imagine. Jesus said, "when you pray, go into your room, close the door, and pray to your Father, who is unseen. Then your Father, who sees what is done in secret will reward you. When you ask—don't keep babbling like pagans, for they think they will be heard because of their many words. Do not be like them, for your Father knows what you have need of before you even ask" (Matthew 6:6-8). As the song says, I got Jesus on the mainline, all I have to do is tell 'em what I want.

I ask—even though the doctors say it's impossible. I ask—because I could never accomplish what Spirit can do for me. I ask—knowing that Spirit will bless me beyond my wildest dreams. I ask for the unborn to manifest in this existence. I ask to give birth to those possibilities that I have not yet embraced. I ask for the unseen to reveal itself to me. I ask and my request itself becomes the catalyst of my change. I ask, and I receive. I ask, knowing that Divine Mind creates the extraordinary out of the ordinary. I ask, realizing that we can walk into our season and be blessed by the goodness of God. I ask keeping in mind what Jesus said in Mark 11:24, "whatever you ask for in prayer, believe that you have received it, and it will be yours."

I decree that I am centered in my blessings.

Where Two or More Are Gathered, There God Is

It's time to gather in God.

We cannot deny that we may not be close physically during social distancing, but we can be closer spiritually. As some say, we are locked in, but God is not locked out. The body of Christ (John 2:19-21) symbolizes humanity's Oneness with God: a temple not limited to space or time or structure but unlimited in the consciousness of faith. Jesus repeatedly taught us that we are made whole by our faith: we are the temple of God. In our bodies, minds, hearts, and souls is the temple—always open and available to be a full expression of God's love.

The true church is a faith that is not confined to religion. The Holy Spirit does not limit itself to Christians, Muslims, Jews, Hindus, or Buddhists but is available to the entire world. The Bible says that all of them were filled with the Holy Spirit (Acts 2:5-11).

"Now there were devout Jews from every nation under heaven living in Jerusalem. And at this sound the crowd gathered and was bewildered, because each one heard them speaking in the native language of each. Amazed and astonished, they asked, 'Are not all these who are speaking Galileans? And how is it that we hear, each of us, in our own native language? Parthians, Medes, Elamites, and residents of Mesopotamia, Judea and Cappadocia, Pontus and Asia, Phrygia, and Pamphylia, Egypt and the parts of Libya belonging to Cyrene, and visitors from Rome, both Jews and proselytes, Cretans and Arabs—in our own languages we hear them speaking about God's deeds of power."

A shared disease is the "tongue" that brought us together and forced us to speak the truth of the love of the Holy Spirit. The Holy Spirit is the Spirit of Wholeness, the Whole Spirit of God in action. As Thich Nhat Hanh said, "the Holy Spirit is the energy of God in us . . . . We know the Holy Spirit as energy and not as notions and words. Wherever there is understanding, the Holy Spirit is there."

In his best-selling book *Think and Grow Rich*, which was written during the depression and first published in 1937, Napoleon Hill encouraged everyone to use the "Power of the Master Mind." Napoleon Hill taught that the best way to access the Master Mind is through "coordination of knowledge and effort, in a spirit of harmony, between two or more people, for the attainment of a definite purpose."

In Matthew 18:12, Jesus put it more simply, saying, "where two or more are gathered in my name, there I am in the midst of them."

I was always taught that "two or more" means at least God and me. However, we define "two," when two or more are in total agreement, it shall be done because we have infused our communion and our connection with the power of faith. We have shifted from the material world to the place where we are no longer bound by the rules of space and time.

Gathering with others makes us more aware and accountable to what we all need, whether articulated or not. Where two or more are gathered, we open our hearts in a new way. We are wired to give—the act of giving of raising another's frequency begins to activate this energy. We can then connect with and raise the frequencies of all energy centers of others, organizing greater frequencies to manifest our good.

*I decree that I am the frequency of God
everywhere present.*

Now is the Time to Return to Spirit

It's time to recognize our oneness with God.

I f we want to experience the power of God healing our bodies, creating new opportunities we could never have imagined before, and having transcendent, mystical experiences—we first need to master the concept of the present moment, the eternal now. Now is the time to be centered in Spirit, which requires that we get beyond the physical world—even beyond time itself. This is where we turn possibility into reality. After all, if you do not get beyond how we have been conditioned to believe the world works, it's impossible to create a new life or a new destiny. So, we must get out of our own way, transcend the memory of ourselves as an identity, and allow something greater than ourselves to take over.

If we focus on fearful thoughts, that is what we experience. The moment we limit ourselves to fearful thoughts, they will trigger the release of even more chemicals in the brain and body that make us continue to feel more fear. The next thing we know, we believe our fear creates feeling, and our feelings are the foundation of our fears, remaining stuck in fear, frustration, and doubt because where we place our attention is what we create for ourselves.

Each moment presents a new opportunity to shift our paradigms, to change the way we think and what we believe, because we can create a blank slate. We always have an amazing opportunity to be present, return from the far country and realize Christ in us as our hope of glory. We can only return to the presence and power of Spirit when we leave the past behind and allow ourselves to be embraced by the love of God.

The Bible tells us that when the prodigal son came home, as soon as his father saw him, he said, "[b]ring forth quickly the best robe and put it on him, and put a ring on his finger, and shoes on his feet. And bring the fatted calf and kill it and let us eat and make merry, for this my son was dead and is alive again. He was lost and now is found." God is saying that if we find our way back to Spirit, our lives will be restored. If we center in Spirit and Truth, we will experience the unlimited sweetness of freedom and realize the unlimited good of the Kingdom of God.

In the story of the prodigal son, we can see the son as representing the human consciousness stuck in the sickness, failure, unhappiness, and inner and outer turmoil of the world. We can see the Father as the perfect wholeness of absolute good. We can see the love of the neighbors as acceptance of our abilities to do even greater things. Returning home is the present moment. Breathing in the present moment, we realize our oneness with God. God does not merely feed us and heal us and bless us and favor us; God gives us a feast; brings out the fatted calf, which is universal substance, life in its fullest, all of the riches that you desire, all of the things that you have been praying for. But we have to leave the far country of doubt; the far country of lack; the far country of limited thinking; the far country of fear; the far country of worry; the far country of dis-ease and be present to the full power of God expressing in, as and through us.

I return from the far country today to Unlimited Source, Divine Mind, the Consciousness of Christ, to the absolute good, to the grace of perfect wholeness, to the image and likeness in which I was made; to the same mind that healed the sick and raised the dead; to the Spirit in which I live and move and have my being; to the truth that unfolds in each moment in every breath that I take—without ceasing.

I decree that the Love of Spirit never ends and is always blessing me and co-creating as me.

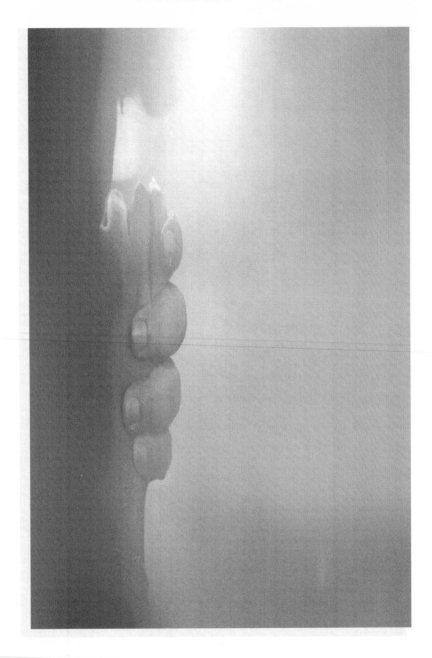

Love One Another

It's time to love without ceasing.

In the First Letter of John, in Chapter 4, Verse 8, John teaches us that "God is love." In the 4th Chapter, the 12th through the 13th Verses, the scripture says, "[n]o one has ever seen God; but if we love one another, God lives in us and His love is made complete in us. We know that we live in Him and He in us, because He has given us His Spirit."

We are here to recognize that the energy of God is available to us and to every person in our midst through the power of love. In the 16th Verse of 1 John Chapter 4, John solidifies the unlimited power of loving when he teaches us "[w]hoever lives in love lives in God, and God in Him," God in her, God as us.

In Isaiah 41:10, God says, "do not fear, for I am with you; do not be dismayed, for I am your God. I will strengthen you and help you with my righteous right hand." Love says there is no need to fear that we will be strengthened every step of the way. There is no need to worry, no need to doubt. This does not mean that we throw caution to the wind, but it does mean that we have sanctuary in the loving power of Spirit.

In Isaiah 43, God says, "Do not fear, for I have redeemed you; I have summoned you by name; you are mine. When you pass through the waters, I will be with you; and when you pass through the rivers, they will not sweep over you. When you walk through the fire, you will not be burned; the flames will not set you ablaze. Since you are precious and honored in my sight, and because I love you, I will give people in exchange for you, nations in exchange for your life. Do not be afraid, for I am with you."

Jephthah crossed Gilead and won the war against the Ammonites because he had a mind stayed on the love of Spirit. With love, the battle is over because we win before the fight begins. This endless source of love emanates in endless directions, at the center of everything that we are. Allow this light of God to remove any impediments, concerns, fears, doubts, thoughts, appearances of dis-ease, despair, worry, and be the loving presence of Spirit. Feel its light and its energy lift you into a new awareness of God present in all that you are.

I decree the love of all that Spirit is.

This is An Opportunity to Change

*It's time to take advantage
of our opportunities.*

I pray not only in reaction to dis-ease, but I affirm our ability to change. 1 Corinthians 15:51 says, "Behold, I tell you a mystery: We shall not all sleep, but we shall all be changed." Crisis creates an opportunity to change. Regardless of where we are in life or how much we've accomplished or failed to accomplish, we can change. We can practice maintaining elevated emotions and changing our energy, shifting the composition of our bodies to make proteins to strengthen our internal defense system.

The outer world is a reflection of our inner consciousness. Abundance is that place in higher consciousness, where water is turned into wine, where fish and loaves are multiplied, where we are made whole. We can affirm that we do not inherit sickness. We can shift from pain to power. We can shift from blindness to vision. We can shift from lame to walking. We can shift from fear to favor. We can shift from ignorance to knowing. We can shift from conquered to conqueror. We can radiate the light of the kingdom within us and shine that light throughout the world. We can shift our consciousness in the power that we all share, the wholeness that we all share—out of which we can create anything.

I decree a new consciousness of abundance and wholeness.

We Dwell in the Secret Place of the Most High

It's time to feel the protection of God.

I want to go back to the 91st Psalm this morning, and study closer what the Psalmist says, which are not merely words of comfort but teach us who we are as Children of the "Most High." The first verse says that if we dwell in the secret place of the Most High, we abide under the shadow of the Almighty. The psalm does not say if we go to the secret place *every now and then*. It does not say if we visit there when we are in trouble. It says if we remain in, live in, dwell in the secret place of the Most High, we will receive the protection of God.

How do we dwell in the secret place of the Most High? We pray daily. We meditate daily. We visualize daily. We study the Word daily. We write, bless others, and stop giving our energy and attention to doubt, fear, worry, stress, and strife, what Jesus called the appearances of things. We affirm with clarity, courage, and boldness about what we want. We speak the truth and believe beyond the appearances of the world. We praise and are grateful for God's good. We abide in the realization that we are co-creators with absolute good.

The Psalmist says I will say of the LORD, He is my refuge and my fortress: my God; in him will I trust. When we trust in God, the word of absolute good becomes a fortress, protection that is greater than anything in the flesh. God is our fortress when locked into a consciousness of Good, locked in a consciousness of Peace, locked in a consciousness of Joy, locked in a consciousness of Prosperity, locked in a consciousness of Health.

The Psalmist says surely he shall deliver thee from the snare of the fowler and from the noisome pestilence. He shall cover thee with his feathers and under his wings shalt thou trust. His truth shall be thy shield and buckler. We walk through challenges, wars, and battles in the world, but Spirit is our shield, and its Truth our buckler. The only way to experience Truth is to make sure that our thoughts are in alignment with the omnipotence of God. The truth is that God is the only power that there is, the knowledge that protects us. The material world is always changing, but Truth is constant.

The Psalmist says thou shalt not be afraid for the terror by night; nor for the arrow that flieth by day; nor for the pestilence that walketh in darkness; nor for the destruction that wasteth at noonday. Daytime refers to troubles that you are consciously aware of, and nighttime refers to those things that are unknown and unsuspected. It does not matter whether we see something in the flesh or not; no one can keep God's good from us. Take back your energy from fear, and instead, see the grace of absolute good.

The Psalmist says a thousand shall fall at thy side, and ten thousand at thy right hand, but it shall not come nigh thee. Only with thine eyes shalt thou behold and see the reward of the wicked. The lesson here is not that God favors us over anyone else, but we are made whole through our faith. God is Spirit. We each can dwell in the secret place of the Most High as long as we dwell in the consciousness of God. Then, we can stroll through the obstacle course that life appears to be, and things may fall near us, break near us, but nothing will harm us.

The Psalmist says, because thou hast made the Lord, which is my refuge, even the Most High, thy habitation, there shall no evil befall thee, neither shall any plague come nigh thy dwelling place. Our homes are, wherever we are, collective points of energy that we can fill with love and light, energy that will not only radiate to the rest of the world but throughout the entire universe. If we pray in one space, we fill that space with so much loving energy that sometimes we can just sit and be blessed by the energy, without even trying to be centered. When we dwell in the consciousness of God, it blesses everything around us.

The Psalmist says he shall give his angels charge over thee, to keep thee in all thy ways. They shall bear thee up in thy hands, lest thou dash thy foot against a stone. You will tread upon the lion and the cobra; you will trample the great lion and the serpent. We will not become a victim of our lives but instead be lifted in higher consciousness as co-creator of greatness. We can call the Most High the quantum realm, absolute good, or unconditional love, or we can call the grace that we surrender to "God." Regardless of what confronts us, the battle is not ours; it is God's, holding us in the protective hands of Spirit.

I breathe in God, and I breathe out I AM. No matter what is before me, whether I am confronted by a lion, a cobra, or a pandemic, I am protected by the love of God I surrender to right now.

I decree the secret place of the "Most High," and in so doing, I renew my commitment to the greatest power that there is.

We Live in God

It's time to be guided by God.

We live in Spirit. In our own heart, we have God, and we live, move, and have our being in all that Spirit is. Within us is a spiritual teacher, who is our counselor and our guide. The most powerful teacher is inside us rather than outside. If we take refuge in this teacher within us, we will never be disappointed. We must love ourselves to recognize the divine in us and see the divine in others. Proverbs 16:9 says, "[p]eople do their best making plans for their lives, but the Eternal guides each step."

In Isaiah 42:16, God says, "I will escort the blind down roads they do not know, guide them down paths they've never seen. I will smooth their passage and light their way." Similarly, Isaiah

49:10 says we "will be fine, never hungry nor thirsty. . . . protected from oppressive heat and the burning sun because the One who loves them—as a mother loves her child—will be their guide."

Jesus says, "[b]ut when He, the Spirit of truth, comes, He will guide you into all the truth. He will not speak on his own; He will speak only what he hears, and he will tell you what is yet to come" (John 16:13). Exodus 13:21 says, "[t]he Eternal went on ahead to guide them during the day in a cloud shaped like a pillar; at night He appeared to them in a fire shaped like a pillar to light their way. So they were able to travel by day and by night." The Prophet Isaiah says (60:19), "[t]he Eternal One will be all the light you ever need."

When we center in the Spirit, the guidance that we need, the "great Helper, the Holy Spirit, in My name to teach you everything and to remind you of all I have said to you" (John 14:26). In Psalm 23:3, the Psalmist says, "he refreshes my soul. He guides me along the right paths for his name's sake." Psalm 25:5 says, "Guide me in your truth and teach me."

We often pressure ourselves to make all decisions in the flesh, but we can let go and be guided in the Spirit.

I decree that I am guided by the divine within.

Leave Your Nets

It's time to leave impossibility.

I n the Book of Matthew, Chapter 4, Verses 18-20, the Bible teaches us that "[as] Jesus was walking by the Sea of Galilee, he saw two brothers, Simon called Peter and his brother Andrew. They were casting a net into the lake, for they were fishermen. 'Come, follow me,' Jesus said, 'and I will make you fishers of men.' And it says, it says that at once they left their nets and followed him." Peter and his brother Andrew were in the midst of their lives, their jobs, their careers, and they didn't even question Jesus; they just stopped what they were doing, and they left. They left their communities; they left their neighborhood; they left their jobs; they left their comfort zones. They left their nets and followed him. So, the question that this presents to us is whether we are to drop our dependence on people, things, and conditions and live totally and completely trusting in God? Now, this should be an even easier question for us because we already know about the resurrection. The disciples had no idea that Jesus was going to be crucified and resurrected

"Come follow me," Jesus said, and I will make you fishers of men. Be in that place of consciousness where we will not say to Jesus, no go on for a season, I have to catch more fish for my family. Be in that consciousness where we won't say to Jesus, it's not the right time, or I prefer to trust in the appearances around me, in doubt and despair. Leaving our nets means that we leave our worries. We leave our doubts. We leave our fears and just step out wholly and entirely on faith.

We leave our nets when we really begin to understand and connect with and resonate with what Jesus said when he told his disciples to stop worrying about what you will eat and what you will drink and what you will wear, and seek first the kingdom of God, and all else will be added.

Jesus is saying no matter what the situation is, no matter what the appearances are, what other people think, or what the newspapers say. Just put me first, and you will get what you need. Just bring me your problems, bring me your challenges, center in the Spirit, and the answers, the good, and the deliverance you need will always be given to you.

When we depend on inexhaustible supply and endless source, we have the luxury of not knowing how our good will take shape. The only thing that we need to do is realize that there may be a limit to what we can do, what we can see, or what we can know, but there is no limit to what God can do. When we leave our nets, we allow God to take over. We trust the infinite possibilities of the Universe, and then, we don't even have to step into our greatness; God will lift us up and put us in our anointed place, at our right time.

As God asked Job: "Do you give the horse its strength or clothe its neck with a flowing mane? It laughs at fear, afraid of nothing. Does the hawk take flight by your wisdom and spread its wings toward the south? Does the eagle soar at your command and build its nest on high?"

When God asked Abraham to sacrifice his beloved son Isaac as a burnt offering, Abraham had to leave his net to trust God and be obedient to what God told him to do. But the scripture says that Abraham got up and saddled his donkey, saddled his pride, stubbornness, and will, took the wood for the burnt offering, and placed it on his son Isaac. Isaac said, "[t]he fire and wood are here, but where is the lamb for the burnt offering?" Abraham answered, "God himself will provide the lamb." God will provide the lamb. God will provide the net. God will give us the extra protection that we need and the escape hatch if necessary. The Bible tells us that when they reached the place God had told him about, Abraham laid Isaac on top of the wood. But when he reached for the knife to slay his son, an angel stopped him because he trusted entirely in God.

"Come follow me," Jesus said, and I will make you fishers of men."

Close your eyes and see yourselves in that consciousness of trust where you are standing right in the midst of this chaos that we could never imagine, and feel the presence of the light of God, of Spirit, of Divine Mind, of Loving Energy, of Everlasting

Perfect Health and Wholeness all around you. Realize the urge to look up from where you are, and for the very first time, look right into the eyes of Jesus. It was as though he was there, all of the time, right in front of you. And when you see Jesus, you see a radiant light of the Universe. You see nothing but absolute good flowing from his eyes and every aspect of his being.

As soon as you see him, you go to him. It is like feeling the true embrace of ever-lasting love, something that you have never felt before. He hugs you, and immediately the worries fall from your soul. Immediately your body is healed. Immediately your errors are forgiven. You just let everything go. You feel the magnitude of Spirit filling your lungs, joints, glands, eyes, muscles, and inner vibrations. See yourself letting go of everyone, every circumstance, everything in your life, every desire, every hope, every challenge, every ailment, every disease, every injury, every fear, every project, every task, everything that isn't Jesus. You release it. You step forward. You let go forever, and you follow him.

I decree that I let go and follow
the Christ within.

Hold the Light

It's time to hold the light of all that Spirit is.

Pastor Paul Carrington sings a song about a little boy whose father told him to wait for him, but while he was waiting, he told him to hold the light. It got late in the evening, but he kept right on holding the light. When the father returned, the little boy said, "Daddy, it rained on me, but I held the light. Some people came by and tried to make me get off the stomp and told me to put the light down, but I listened to what you said, so I wouldn't move. I just stayed here, and I held the light. And a third group came by, and they laughed at me, but I kept holding the light."

Holding the light means that we are not merely radiating the light for ourselves; we shine the light for others. Jesus said in Matthew 5:14, "You are the light of the world. A city that is set on a hill cannot be hid. Neither do men light a candle and put it under a bushel, but on a candlestick; and it giveth light unto all that are in the house. Let your light shine so before men that they may see your good works." He does not mean our personal accomplishments. He means the light that radiates through us as the true power of Spirit shining despite our desire to let go. Someone else on the path might have fallen, but the little boy kept holding the light. We are being called to hold the light, to trust that that part of us that knows to hold on—even when we want to quit.

Holding the light is the realization that we have a choice to connect with the presence and power of the light of Spirit. We can allow that light to radiate throughout our bodies and see them whole and well, be lifted in the power of our light, and realize that we are not limited in the light but can send the infinite reach of our light worldwide. As our Father said, never let go of the light. We can use our light as a beacon for all of those whom we meet.

I decree that I will keep holding the light.

Meditate to Change Your Lives

It's time to be still.

I f all your attention and energy is tied up in your outer world of people, objects, things, places, and time, there is no energy left in your inner world of thoughts and feelings. Therefore, the stronger the emotion you are addicted to, the more you will focus on that person, object, place, or circumstance in your outer world—giving away most of your creative energy and causing you to feel and think equal to everything you know. It becomes challenging to think or feel in any new way when you are addicted to your outer world. And it's possible that you can become addicted to all the people and things in your life that are causing all your problems in the first place. That's how you give your power away and mismanage your energy.

So, one of the questions we ask ourselves is, "How much of your creative energy is tied up in guilt, hatred, resentment, lack, or fear?" The truth is that you could be using all that energy to re-create a new destiny. To do that, you're going to have to get beyond all of those things in your outer world by taking your attention off them. That's why we use meditation to change our internal state.

This allows us to break from our associations to everybody, everyone, everything, everywhere, and every time long enough to journey within. Once you overcome your emotional body and take your attention off everything known to you in your outer world, you call your energy back to you, breaking the bonds with your past-present reality (which has stayed the same).

You will have to make the transition from being somebody to being nobody—which means you take your attention off your body, your pain, and your hunger. You will have to go from being someone to being no one (taking your attention off your identity as a partner, a parent, and an employee). You will stop focusing on something to focusing on nothing. You will forget your cell phone, e-mails, and coffee to nothing and nowhere. Your understanding of time will change from the assumption that time is linear to realizing there is no past, present, or future.

In the book of Joshua, the first chapter, the eighth verse, it says, "[t]his Book of the Law shall not depart from your mouth, but you shall meditate in it day and night, that you may observe to do according to all that is written in it. For then, you will make your way prosperous, and then you will have good success." The

Psalmist says in Psalm 119:99, "I have more understanding than all my teachers, for your testimonies are my meditation."

The purpose of our meditation is to affirm in our consciousness that which is true of God. "In God, I am now a perfect child. I am strong, confident, and capable. I can do all that needs to be done. I am one with all-sufficient substance, so I am secure and fearless." These things may be urgent needs in your experience. But the Father knows even before you ask—and it is the Father's good pleasure to give you the Kingdom. Thus, don't waste your time asking for help. It is already yours. Claim it. Call it forth into expression. Speak the Word of Truth.

"But when thou prayest, enter into the inner chamber and shut thy door." This is Jesus' teaching of silence, the dynamic concept of deep prayer. In a very real sense, much that we think of as prayer is a preparation for prayer. It is the process of resolving the conflicts of the mind so that we can "Be still, and know that I am God" (Psalm 46:10). Jesus is telling us, we should dig deeper into who we are As we grow in understanding the Truth of our relationship with God, as we begin to see ourselves in the light of our divinity, prayer becomes an experience in the silence. We put the words behind us.

The most powerful thing we can do is be silent and breathe in our connection to God, what I call absolute good, Spirit, and when we do—our good flows to us with ease.

Sit in the silence with a mantra this week, one minute or two minutes—as long as you can and commit to it each day. Be still as the Psalmist says and know that you are God. You are an heir to the throne.

I decree that I will meditate daily.

We Are Moving Through a Portal of Re-Birth

It's time to move beyond the pandemic.

What changes are we making as we move through the portal of the pandemic? This is a question for all of us. No matter what, we will not be the same as when we entered. We will be reborn.

The portal that we walk through will allow us to realize the sanctity of home and shelter that have blessed us in our times of need. Bless your home here and now, and realize it's a sacred place. Clean, repair, and restore its beauty. Honor the wings of Spirit that have sheltered, protected, and kept you safe.

The portal we walk through will strengthen our immunity. We will remain strong. Our bodies will repair themselves. Bless your body. Eat whole foods that contribute to its repair: exercise and stretch. Remain obedient to the guidance of Spirit and the benefit of resilience, always making you strong.

As God told Joshua, "I will give you every place where you set your foot, as I promised Moses" (Joshua 1:3). God told Joshua, "As I was with Moses, so I will be with you; I will never leave you nor forsake you" (Joshua 1:5). "I will . . . exalt you in the eyes of all Israel" (Joshua 3:7). I will give you the good that I gave Moses.

Be reborn centered in the love of Spirit, without second-guessing its inexhaustible source and unlimited supply. There is nothing that you will long for; nothing that will not manifest for you; nothing that will not bless you; nothing that you will not be able to uplift as the glory of God.

I called you, Spirit says to us. I know that you are not faint of heart. You have been obedient. You have done the work. You have run without getting weary. You have stayed the course. So, this is what I'm going to do for you. When you cross the Jordan, when you go through the portal and make it to the other side, you will stand in the light of truth and be lifted in the power of your greatness.

I decree a light of truth through the portal.

We Have a Covenant with God

It's time to reap the benefits of God's good.

O ne of the messages from the Bible is the power of the 40-day period for transforming your life. Forty symbolizes completion, "as long as it takes." In the story of Noah, it rained for 40 days and 40 nights. Moses was on the mountain for 40 days and 40 nights. The Israelites spied on Canaan for 40 days. Goliath taunted the Israelites for 40 days. Elijah traveled for 40 days and 40 nights to the Mountain of God. Jonah's prophecy was that Ninevah would be overthrown in 40 days. Jesus fasted for 40 days and 40 nights. Jesus walked the earth for 40 days after he was resurrected.

You will find that the old is released at the end of these 40-day periods, and the new comes forth. For example, Genesis 9 teaches us that after Noah's 40 days and nights on the ark, God blessed Noah and his sons, saying to them, "[b]e fruitful and increase in number and fill the earth." And God even blessed them with a covenant that would be for every living creature for generations to come. A rainbow was set in the clouds as a sign of the covenant between God and earth.

As Marlon and I walked the other day, we saw the rainbows drawn by children in the windows. When I did some research, it appears that the teachers were telling the children to draw rainbows to inspire hope, which is phenomenal because rainbows have always inspired hope. Rainbows are a covenant with God. A covenant is a contract, an agreement that humanity will be restored. But contracts are not one-sided; both sides give.

The seven colors of the solar spectrum are produced by different rates of vibration of universal energy, which makes the vibrations visible. If we are like Noah, obedient to God's guidance, we are not destroyed by hostile conditions. When we are obedient, the perfect principles of unity and God will be forever established.

Only when we transgress the law, when a great reaction sets in and a condition shakes our foundation, like a pandemic, do we look obediently to God, suddenly awakened. This awakening is represented by Noah, through whom the seed of a new state of consciousness is saved. The truly awakened will not fear the flood but learn from the cleansing it brings about.

We are being forced to heed this lesson of Noah whose name symbolizes rest, to learn to let go of physical tenseness and material things and open our minds to divine intelligence, what some call the quantum realm, some call it the kingdom of God, some call the vortex, some call grace, some call love.

The ark represents a positive, saving state of consciousness, which agrees with or forms a covenant with higher consciousness or Christ consciousness to realize our oneness with Spirit. We sail gently above the flood of error thoughts with spiritual surrender: I am one with love. I am one with absolute good. I am one with perfect health and wholeness.

Only when our own waters of negation subside do we walk forth and populate the "earth" with a new consciousness of Spirit. This is the portal of new growth and enlightenment. The ark represents the new body that the mind spiritually projects.

What will you bring on your ark? What are you taking into the portal of the new day? What do you need to leave behind? If we cannot make these necessary decisions for our personal transformation and for those around us, this cleansing will not be complete. We are at the forefront of cosmic evolution, which starts with the decisions we make for ourselves.

We must examine ourselves. We must look inside and come to terms with what's there. We must take responsibility for our own thoughts and beliefs and be obedient and accountable to ourselves. No one can do this for us. We must take our values into the ark, the love through which all is created, integrity, compassion, community, and truth.

Leave negativity and despair, and bring the projects that God, Spirit, Divine Mind has blessed us to give others.

I decree that I release lack of discipline, hopelessness, doubt, and negativity.

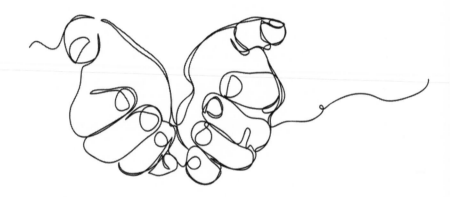

We Liberate Ourselves Through Forgiveness

It's time to reap the liberation of forgiveness.

I
n Genesis 50:1-3, it says that "Joseph fell on his father's face and wept over him, and kissed him. And Joseph commanded his servants, the physicians, to embalm his father. Forty days were required for him, for such are the days required for those who are embalmed." There, the 40-day period symbolized laying aside the past: forgiveness, releasing, and letting go. The truth is that we don't harm other people; we harm ourselves when we don't forgive. When blaming someone, condemning someone, fretting about someone, getting angry at someone, cursing someone, thinking negatively about someone,

we are not punishing them; we are only punishing ourselves. To move forward, we must forgive.

Matthew 18:21-22 says, "[t]hen Peter came to Jesus and asked, 'Lord, how many times shall I forgive my brother or sister who sins against me? Up to seven times?' Jesus answered, 'I tell you, not seven times, but seventy-seven times.'" Jesus said that we should not just forgive 70 times, but 77 times. In other words, we remain complete, in a perpetual state of forgiveness. Seven is the divine law of perfection. But sometimes, we become so attached to our anger that it is challenging to release, which is why we cannot move forward. We become emotionally invested in our drama. We start creating the stories, the rationalizations, the justifications, and we do not want to let go of them. They become the way that we define ourselves. We are reluctant, if not afraid, to leave our old miserable, condemning, unforgiving selves. The irony is that only by forgiving do we push past our self-imposed boundaries and tap the unlimited source of divine possibilities.

In healing ourselves and boosting our immune system, forgiveness is not something we merely give; forgiveness is a gift. Forgiveness is something we give ourselves. The pivotal portal that we are witnessing requires the ultimate sacrifice, which is not giving to the flesh but surrendering to the Spirit. We need to leave our baggage on the other side of the portal and forgive whatever we need to forgive here and now. We do not need any negativity or poison, wherever it comes from, blocking our good.

Forgiveness has been described by some as a mental bath—letting go of something that can only poison us within. Science supports that forgiveness results in fewer symptoms of psychological distress, such as feelings of nervousness, restlessness, and sadness. Scientists say that unforgiveness compromises the immune system at many levels, throwing off the production of essential hormones and disrupting the way our cells fight off infections, bacteria, and other physical diseases. We must release those toxins passing away, while remembering and reaching toward revitalizing what lies before us.

Here and now, I forgive every inappropriate touch, gesture, and word hurled at me. I forgive everything that someone meant for evil—because God meant it for good. I forgive Adam and Eve for eating that fruit; I forgive Cain for killing Abel; I forgive Lot's wife for turning back; I forgive every hater, every false accuser, every repeated lie because I am not carrying anything or anybody or any condition into this new consciousness because I am going to step into my greatness. I am going to claim my victory.

I forgive myself for not being perfect. I forgive myself for wasting time. I forgive myself for going backward instead of going forward. I forgive myself for trying to do the best that I can without success. I forgive myself for not seizing the possibilities that life has in store for me. I forgive myself for holding onto the past.

I dig deep down in my soul, deep down into the recesses of my mind, and I pull out every single idle resentment that I might be holding onto. And as soon as I identify it—I swiftly say, I send you love. I forgive you. I release you. I see you achieving great success. I bless you. I bless your father. I bless your sister. I bless your entire family. But most importantly, I let you go.

I decree that I forgive you, and I set me free.

We Each Have a Divine Role

It's time to recognize our divine role.

Traditionally, Good Friday is set aside for the religious observance of the crucifixion hour. The unfortunate thing about the Gospels is that the writers emphasized the crucifixion instead of Jesus' life. To set the record straight—Judas was one of Jesus' closest friends. Jesus believed in him, saw great possibilities in him, personally selected him as one who could be of great help to the cause. And let us never forget that, like all the disciples, Judas gave up everything to follow Jesus.

Jesus did not condemn Judas. He seemed almost compassionate as He pointed him out—almost as if it were a matter of an assignment that someone had to have. As we read the story, Jesus seems to be almost an accessory to the "crime" of Judas. The text states that Jesus announced that he who would receive the sop was the one who would betray Him. And it says that "Satan" entered Judas when he dipped his hand into the dish with that of Jesus. Jesus then turned to Judas and said, "What thou doest, do quickly." It was almost as if He had given him the charge: "This is your job, go and do it."

The disciples had not seemed to catch it, but Jesus had long known and often stated that this was to be his destiny. It was a destiny that He chose. He had a choice, but He chose to go through this experience as the means of revealing the great Truth of the resurrection principle to man.

One of the most misunderstood of the dramatic "Seven Last Words" is "Eli, Eli, lama sabachthani" (Matt. 27:46). This has always been translated, "My God, my God, why hast thou forsaken me." George Lamsa, a world-renowned Syrian scholar and translator of the Bible, said that Jesus was actually saying, "My God, my God, for this was I kept—I am fulfilling my destiny. I am on the way through the dark hour to the great demonstration of resurrection and the complete fulfillment of man's divinity." Jesus forgave those who crucified Him and those who taunted Him. He said, "Forgive them for they know not what they are doing" (Luke 23:34).

Judas was a tool, an instrument, playing a destiny-chosen role in the dramatic portrayal of a great lesson. Judas, then, must have had a choice. What led him to accept this role? It may be that Judas accepted the role, as Jesus those many years ago accepted the mantle of the Messiah—choosing to fulfill the prophecy of man's divinity. Judas may have become the one—

not because of his weakness, but because of his strength, coupled with an erroneous concept of Jesus' mission.

Judas went to the chief priests and sold Jesus for thirty pieces of silver. It was a tiny sum. Judas came from a wealthy background. Thus, the money meant nothing. Jesus made no effort to defeat the act of Judas because what Judas did, allowed Jesus to be resurrected. Jesus had to go to the cross to prove His liberation from the physical realm, so that the full demonstration of eternal life could manifest.

There is a Judas state of mind in us all, one that seeks opportunities to an instrument of change, one that allows us to bear witness to the most challenging truth.

I decree the truth that what appears bad reveals our greatest blessing.

Claim Your Power in Galilee

It's time to go to Galilee.

Before he was crucified, the scripture teaches us, in Matthew 26:32 and Mark 14:28, that Jesus prophesized, saying, "after I have risen, I will go ahead of you into Galilee." We tend to gloss over the scripture's repeated references to Galilee. If we look closely, we will see that in the first chapter of Mark, it says, in the 14th verse, Jesus went into "Galilee," proclaiming the good news of God. Jesus was walking beside the Sea in "Galilee" when he saw Simon and his brother Andrew casting their nets (Mark 1:16). Jesus went throughout Galilee, teaching in synagogues, proclaiming the good news of the kingdom, and healing every disease and sickness among the people. In Galilee, at a wedding in Cana, where he demonstrated his first miracle, turning water into wine. It was in Galilee that Jesus demonstrated his second miracle, healing the son of a royal official.

In the Gospels, we learn that after Jesus had arisen, he told the women who saw him near his tomb, "Do not be afraid. Go and tell my brothers to go to Galilee; there they will see me." When they saw him, Jesus said, I am with you always, to the very end of the age." (Matthew 28:7-10, 20; Mark 17:7, 15-20; John 21:1). It was in Galilee where the disciples could not catch any fish, Jesus appeared, and said "Throw your net on the right side of the boat and you will find some." When they did, they could not haul the net in because of the large number of fish. (John 21:6).

Galilee is not just a place, not just a mountain where Jesus worshipped, not just the setting where his miracles took place, but the place in our consciousness that is filled with Christ. In Galilee, we embrace the consciousness of Christ, realizing that we are not in it but it is in us, not a place in time or space but receptive to the Divine Mind that created all that is and made us in its image and likeness.

Come, Jesus said, come to Galilee, center in your highest consciousness, and there you will find me, lifted in the realm of the greater things that you are here to do.

I decree that I am lifted in Galilee.

Christ is Resurrected in Us

It's time to resurrect the Christ in us.

The Bible says in Matthew 28 that after the Sabbath, at dawn on the first day of the week, Mary Magdalene and the other Mary went to look at the tomb. There was a violent earthquake, for an angel of the Lord came down from heaven and, going to the tomb, rolled back the stone, and sat on it. His appearance was like lightning, and his clothes were white as snow. The guards were so afraid of him that they shook and became like dead men. The angel said to the women, do not be afraid, for I know that you are looking for Jesus, who was crucified. He is not here; he has risen, just as he said. Come and see the place where he lay. Then go quickly and tell his disciples he has risen from the dead. The angel told the women, "do not be afraid, for I know that he has risen."

"He has risen" means that He has transformed beyond the flesh into eternal life. It means that He has died to the physical, but His Spirit lives forever. It means that when we call Him, He will answer. When we need a way out of no way, we can just say Jesus! He will never leave us nor forsake us. He will deliver us and show us our salvation.

Someone once posed the question to me: do you think Jesus never existed? I had never really thought about it, but I could feel the answer to the question at that moment. I could feel that something in me say, well, I know one thing, I don't care what nobody else thinks; I know that Jesus lives for me. I have had my share of struggle, been on my death bed, but I am grateful that I know Jesus. I know the roads and the paths, the turns and the openings where I can find Him. I am with you, Jesus says because he rose. John 11:25-26 says, "I am the resurrection and the life. He who believes in me will live, even though he dies, and whoever lives and believes in me will never die." He said, "I am the way and the truth and the life."

If you want to understand it scientifically, we can say Jesus formed a spiritual zone with the earth's atmosphere from which He penetrated and united with the quantum realm. If you want to think about it theologically, you can say Jesus was crucified, died, and buried but rose again. If you want to ponder it historically, you can say, well, some say there was an earthquake, and when they went in the tomb, burial linens were all that remained. If you want to marshal it metaphysically, you can say well—he lives in the spiritual ethers of this world, and he is in constant contact with those who raise their thoughts to his vibration. For me, the only thing I need is to feel in my heart, know in my mind, and embrace with my soul, that I know Jesus and that Jesus' story—is my story because Jesus lives in me.

We need spiritual connection more than physical communion. I have eaten of Jesus' body, as He said I am the bread, the divine substance, and the manna always there to feed you. Would you partake of this bread here and now with me? I drank of his body, the blood of the covenant, the divine energy of life— the blood that is the consciousness of love. Would you drink of his eternal and living water today? Would you share in a virtual communion, tasting the essence of Jesus in every cell of your being? Would you be able to drink the miracles that flow through the Holy Spirit like supernatural blood? Would you walk with Him on a new water of faith?

Would you put on the new robe that your Father has given you and envision, prophecy, and deliver beyond the expanse of your soul into the secret place of the Most High? Would you open your mind and realize that Jesus has always been here—knowing what you want—before you even ask? Would you be resurrected in a new season of faith—going beyond what you used to know, lifted out of the depths of your self-imposed limitations, and answer His call—and that is Christ in Us Our Hope of Glory! Christ in Us Our Amazing Grace! Christ in Us—the First and the Last! Christ is He who stands at the door and knocks, He whose voice we hear, He who has invited us in, He who has offered a seat with Him on the throne of grace, the gift of spiritual consciousness.

I decree that Christ lives in me.

I am Creator of the Unseen

It's time to create.

In John 20, it says Thomas would not believe in the resurrection until he saw proof. But Jesus paid him a visit and provided him with proof, saying, "Thomas, because you have seen Me, you have believed. Blessed are those who have not seen and yet have believed." Thomas stands for the intellect, that part of us that needs physical proof.

There are prayer studies providing proof, like the one conducted in July 2000 by Israeli doctor Leonard Leibovici. He conducted a study involving 3,393 hospital patients to see whether prayer could impact their condition. He randomly designated half the patients to have prayers for them, while the other half were not prayed for. He established that the prayed-for had a decrease in fever and a shorter hospitalization time. Also, deaths were not as bad in the prayed-for group.

The other proof was that those praying were not praying for patients who were infected in 2000. Unbeknownst to them, they were praying for people ill from 1990 to 1996, four to ten years before the experiment. The prayed-for patients got better during the 1990s from the experiment conducted years later. The patients who were prayed for in 2000 all showed measurable changes in health, but those changes took effect years before. A statistical analysis of this experiment proved that these effects were far beyond coincidence and that prayers not only affect our present or future, but they can impact our past as well.

Many ridicule this science as a joke. But it still provides proof that all potentials exist simultaneously. Our thoughts and feelings affect all aspects of life, beyond both space and time. This is another reason to hold a clear intention of what you want but leave the "how" details to the unpredictable quantum field. Let it orchestrate an event in your life in a way that is just right for you. If you are going to expect anything, expect the unexpected. Surrender, trust, and let go of how the desired event will unfold.

I decree that all possibilities exist.

I Am One With the Holy Spirit

It's time to hear and obey Spirit.

Romans 5:5 says God's love was poured into our hearts through the Holy Spirit. Infinite love is always here, pouring within our souls continuously. Acts 1:8 says you will receive power when the Holy Spirit comes on you. Take a moment and feel the pure power you have with the Holy Spirit, which puts our enemies, doubts, and fears under our feet (Mark 12:36).

Jesus said, "[p]eace be with you! As the Father has sent me, I am sending you" (John 20:19-22). And with that, He breathed on them and said, "Receive the Holy Spirit." If we really knew and worked with the Holy Spirit, our worries would be reduced if not eliminated. John 14:26 says, "the advocate, the Holy Spirit, whom the Father will send in my name, will teach you all things and will remind you of everything I have said to you."

As 1 Corinthians 6:19 says: "do you not know that your bodies are temples of the Holy Spirit, who is in you, whom you have received from God?" I am the servant of the Holy Spirit, carrying out its divine direction. I receive it. I wear it. I am covered by the word of God, and in the word, the sustenance of unlimited good blesses my mind, body, and soul. Through the Holy Spirit, I bless everyone I meet. I am filled with new grace, acknowledging Spirit in me. The battle is not in the flesh but in the Holy Spirit of Absolute Good, which is the only power.

I decree that I am blessed with the Holy Spirit.

The Truth Makes Me Free

It's time to know the truth.

Jesus said you "shall know the truth, and the truth shall make you free" (John 8:32). The truth is that there is no law of retribution in God. Both the causes and the effects function in a realm outside the kingdom of God-consciousness. Thus, no matter the causes or the karmic debt, the effects can be dissolved by "knowing the Truth," by raising our consciousness above the level of sin and its atonement. Paul says, "[t]here is therefore now no condemnation to them that are in Christ Jesus. For the law of the Spirit of life in Christ Jesus made me free from the law of sin and of death" (Romans 8:1).

When we are one with Spirit, we are free from bondage to the flesh, our debt is canceled, and we begin to know and experience the truth of life. This is the quantum realm of absolute good. This is the truth that shall make you free. Prayer is not a matter of cajoling God for release from some karmic debt. The higher law of Spirit supersedes the lower laws of the mental and physical planes. This is not so strange when we see it in the light of progress in science. One hundred years ago, it was thought to be a scientific fact that nothing heavier than air could fly. Today, we have planes and spaceships, not by breaking the law of gravity but by discovering how gravity can be transcended.

The payment of a karmic debt can be satisfied through the salvation of rising above the consciousness from which the misconduct was committed into the freedom of spiritual understanding where we go forth and "sin no more" (John 8:11). In effect, Jesus says forget about that speck you found in someone else's eye and change your own level of consciousness (Matthew 7:3; Luke 6:41). Manifest the truth that miracles are always available to you, as a fundamental function of your higher level of consciousness.

I decree that I am lifted in the truth
that sets me free.

I See the World Rightly

It's time to see what is right.

John 21:4-6 says Jesus said to the disciples while fishing, "Friends, haven't you any fish?" They said, "No," and He said, "Throw your net on the right side of the boat and you will find some." When they did, they could not haul the net in because of the large number of fish. They threw their nets on the right side, the side where the pure power of Spirit is always protecting us. The 91st Psalm says: "Thousands may fall at your left hand [but] and tens of thousands [will fall] at your right." Matthew 25:31-35 says: "he will put the sheep on his right" and only to those on the right will the King say, "Come, you who are blessed by my Father; take your inheritance, the kingdom prepared for you since the creation of the world."

On the right side of God, we do what is right, think what is right, are redeemed in all righteousness, wear the right robes of inexhaustible supply and perfect health, take our divine inheritance, and are blessed in its favor of endless supply, are in a consciousness where God's good never ever runs out. We see and thus experience the world rightly.

In the 16th Psalm, the Psalmist says: "In thy presence is fulness of joy; at thy right hand there are pleasures always." At the right hand is the right realization of the presence of God's good. The "left-sided realm of thinking" only sees physical results. The right lens sees beyond the flesh to the kingdom in which we dwell in the Spirit. We must see the world rightly.

When we pray, we need to pray that we see rightly, see past the appearances blocking God, blocking our ability to haul in the fish from the right side of a complete acceptance of our divine inheritance, see the blessings, see the kingdom that is our birthright. See the world that dwells within you, the kingdom that is neither here nor there but is within you: your consciousness, your soul's oneness with the infinite supply, a kingdom where we co-create with God's unlimited good, and we manifest success—not from worry but by casting our nets on the RIGHT SIDE and reaping the righteousness that sees beyond appearances to the pure power of Spirit.

I decree to see rightly.

I Reap the Blessings of the Kingdom

It's time to reap our blessings.

In John 4: 35-38, Jesus says, "[d]o you not say, 'Four months more and then the harvest'? I tell you, open your eyes and look at the fields! They are ripe for harvest. Even now the reaper draws his wages, even now he harvests the crop for eternal life, so that the sower and the reaper may be glad together. Thus, the saying 'One sows and another reaps' is true. I sent you to reap what you have not worked for. Others have done the hard work, and you have reaped the benefits of their labor." What is there to reap of God's good that is greater than eternal blessings? Eternal blessings are peace, prosperity, love, strength, kindness, and compassion. Blessings increase when we give. Through giving, we reap our greatest harvest.

We reap God's good, even while old structures and paradigms collapse. We do not have to face change with fear or anger, but with the resilience of children given no more than we can bear. Only through change can the new evolve. We reap a future with a new faith of medicine that will heal us, sustain, and uplift us in unexpected ways. We will move through these days filled with the grace of new discoveries, innovations, and advancements, reaping the consciousness through which God's grace flows. We reap the pure presence of the wholeness of God and the divine mind of endless ideas.

Paul told the Corinthians, "God is able to make all grace abound to you, so that in all things at all times, having all that you need, you will abound in every good work" (2 Corinthians 9:8-11). God's expression in and as us is so great; we always reap more than we sow, especially when we need the mercy of grace. We return to new consciousness from the far country, putting on the new robe and ring of endless grace. Our divine inheritance is the harvest of love intricately intertwined with a compassionate movement through the portal of suffering to a new day. Let us hold firmly, without wavering, to the faith that we profess. Let us walk into this season and be more than a witness. Let us be a conqueror. Let us sow without fear as we reap the good that is always ours.

I decree that I reap the good that is mine

Power Creates in Us As Each Moment

It's time to celebrate the power of each moment.

Right now, in this very instant, the Universe is blessing us with so much good, so much joy, so much love, so much abundance, so much success, so much wisdom that we cannot even begin to imagine it. Right now, right here, we are living, moving, and having our being in unlimited source, infinite possibility, and inexhaustible supply. Right now, we have the choice to move beyond the confines of fear, beyond the belief of lack, beyond suffering and doubt—to be the fullest and most complete expression of God that we desire. Right now, in this instant, we are One with the pure potential of Absolute Good, which is so good that it is hard for us to name it. We call it God. We call it Love. We call it the Holy Ghost. We call it Spirit, but it is difficult to name the power that resides in us and celebrates us each moment.

Eckhart Tolle said, "Whatever the present moment contains, accept it as though you have chosen it. Work with it—not against it. Make it your friend and your ally—not your enemy—and you will miraculously change your life."

I saw a movie called *Source Code*—and without giving the plot away, I can say that it's about a soldier employed to find a bomber by traveling back 8 minutes in time—through "the Source Code." He had to re-live the same 8 minutes again and again to identify the bomber. The lesson from the movie, what it really makes us think about, is his ability to alter life each time he experienced those 8 minutes. It makes us realize the importance of 8 minutes—the experience that we can have in a single slice of life, a moment that we live in. What the soldier could do that we cannot do is experience the present moment more than once. By experiencing the present moment more than once, the soldier began to value every second, every moment, every breath that he had, every conversation, every person, every observation, every relationship that crossed his path.

Imagine what would happen if we really believed that we could direct the course of our lives, that we could honor each moment and benefit from every situation that we face. We would do things differently. We wouldn't waste the pure potential spiritual ethers by planting seeds of doubt or despair or hopelessness because we really would believe that the God expressing as us is in charge. So, we wouldn't sweat the small stuff. Like Kehinde

Wiley, we would paint on a larger canvas and create from the infinite source that never hinders us. We would realize that there is no need to look to the left or to the right but only in the center where God is, where our life journey thrives on each step we take in the moment.

Every moment is our resurrection. Every moment has the power to cure us, heal us, prosper us, uplift us, to transform us because we are always God's expression creating through us. Every moment is waiting for us to claim God. Every moment is waiting for us to realize that we can turn challenges into opportunities, to turn separation into community, to turn corruption into service, to turn materialism into generosity, to turn ignorance into knowledge—to become aware that we have the same Christ in us that Jesus had in Him.

We don't have to wait for a better day; better days are here; better moments are now; we are already blessed with the gifts and talents that we desired for ourselves. Our tests have been passed. Our goals have been reached. Our books have been sold. Our treasures have been uncovered. The only thing that the Universe is waiting for is for us to claim them. Time is the obstacle that we place in front of dreams to contain them. We create the struggle and the journey and the path and the course; we create the time that it takes, but the truth is that our good is co-creating with us in every instant.

The Book of Revelations says God has placed before us an open door that no one can shut. We choose how your world will unfold. We choose to move mountains and make a difference.

We choose to expand beyond the world of flesh into the infinite realm of Spirit. We choose to focus on being One with God. We choose to surrender—not to your weakest but your greatest. We choose here and now at this moment to stop limiting ourselves. There is no time-space dimension to God's Good. The moment that we are in doesn't worry about mistakes or failure. This moment is not afraid of walking the water. This moment can multiply fish and bread. This moment can trouble the water. This moment calls it all good. We are being called to a new understanding of truth. We are being taught that a new door has opened. There is nothing but good paved on the road before us. We just have to claim it. Our challenges are but the doors opening to power in us that we cannot even begin to imagine.

I decree the greatness of this moment.

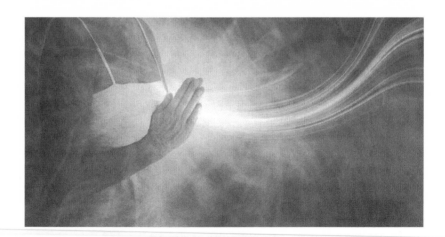

I Center in
Living Water

It's time to sip living water.

I want to start with a meditation that will allow you to lift your consciousness in the Spirit. The energy of light embodies us but also is us. As we close our eyes, we find ourselves connecting beyond body, time, and space to our light of eternity and grace. Moving from our feet to ankles to legs to our first energy center of our creativity, this divine wellspring of Eden giving birth.

We see the light throughout our bodies. Our light radiates through our second energy center, our Abraham center of digestion and elimination, process, and release through the energy of faith, judging our environment not by appearances but by righteous judgment. Our light emanates from our third energy center located in the pit of our gut, our stomach, our solar plexus, Our Israel center of spiritual thought rising to unite us with the Joseph center of enlightenment, illuminated through our imagination. Our light fills our fourth energy center, heart, lungs, and thymus, with God's full expression of love carrying all twelve of our faculties, the sons of Israel. The light of love lifts us above the mediocrity of stress, pain, and desire into our fifth energy center of liberation, located in the center of our throat and thyroid, expressing the light of Moses, up from the wilderness into the Promised Land. We rise through the light of liberation into the sixth energy of awareness, the pineal gland, the third eye, the center of David's grace. The light of grace moves us into the seventh energy center of Solomon, the pituitary gland of wisdom, providing balance, harmony with all things. The light of wisdom enters the energy of Ka, Christ's conscious connection to all that is, oneness with absolute good.

In the light, we draw all good to us, and we feel gratitude for this good, and as we increase our vibrations, we send energy for others to do the same. In the light, we find ourselves in living water. In John 4:10-11, when asked for a drink from a Samaritan woman, it says that a woman of Samaria came to draw water. Jesus said, "[w]hoever drinks of this water will thirst again, but whoever drinks of the water that I shall give him will never thirst. But the water that I shall give him will become in him a fountain of water springing up into everlasting life."

The scripture says, "[o]ut of his heart will flow rivers of living water" (John 7:37-38). Living water is the sea in which our higher consciousness dwells: the sea of abundant, omnipresent, eternal life, the universal life flow. This sea of living water is the quantum, the realm of infinite possibility: a quantum (or unified) field is an invisible field of energy and information—or you could say a field of intelligence or consciousness—that exists beyond space and time. Nothing physical or material exists there. It is beyond anything you can perceive with your senses, filled with infinite amounts of energy vibrating beyond the physical world of matter and beyond our senses—invisible waves of energy available for us to use in creation, the state in which all possibilities exist.

In living water, this endless, vast space as awareness, there are no bodies, no people, no objects, no places, and no time. Instead, infinite unknown possibilities exist as energy. When you take your attention off objects and places in the physical environment, you are in nothing and nowhere. Finally, if you take your attention off linear time (which has a past and a future), you are in no time—you are in the present moment, in which all possibilities in the quantum field exist.

When you are in the present moment, you get out of your own way. As you become pure consciousness, when there is a vibrational match between your energy and any potential that already exists in the unified field, you begin to draw that new experience to you. You do not have to work to bring what you want to manifest to you, and you do not have to go anywhere to get it (that's changing matter with matter). You must become pure consciousness (nobody, no one, nothing, nowhere, no time) and change your energy—the electromagnetic signal you are broadcasting—and then you will draw that future experience right to you (changing energy into matter).

You must align your energy and your emotion with what you want to experience. If you stay in the lower energy and emotions of the past or something you do not want to experience, you will continue to draw that energy to you. You essentially get out of the way. When you are surprised by an unknown experience that seems like it came out of nowhere, it is because you created it in nowhere. Something appeared out of nothing because you created it in nothing. And it can happen in no time if you create it in the realm beyond linear time—that is the quantum field, where there is no time; that is living water, through which all good flows.

I decree that I will drink living water.

The Power of God Radiates as Us

It's time to call on zeal.

I n *God is a Brown Girl Too,* one of the poems I wrote reads: *Who will discover the bones of the plain brown girl, whose skull is as old as time, buried deep in the recesses of prayers long forgotten, older than Lucy, older than Eve's mother, older than dirt? Who will look long enough into her empty sockets? Who will dare to see themselves gazing there? Who will find the courage to lift their legacy out of the realm of the forgotten and speak the truth once again? Not that we are looking for God, but oh, that we have found Her.* These words uplift the truth that the power that is our birthright is not limited to a single race, creed, sexual expression, or other demographic. God represents the absolute good in all of us. Yet, the message is that we must recognize God's power in the most marginalized, if we acknowledge it at all.

> *who will discover*
> *the bones of the plain brown girl*
> *whose skull is as old as time*

The bones of our mother's mother's mothers thousands of years ago are not merely a legacy of struggle or trauma, but represent the ancient wisdom and power that we all share. We need to re-discover who we really are, and remember we are co-creators of Spirit.

> *buried deep in the recesses*
> *of prayers long forgotten older than Lucy*
> *older than Eve's mother*
> *older than dirt*

Are you taking time to give thanks for endless supply, or are you begging because you can't begin to conceive just how good God is as you? The "force" is with us: our ability to communicate, shape, produce, lift, design, and build is in our souls, but most of us have forgotten it. Jesus gave us the truth that can set us free. Are you tapping the truth, now and forever, to emerge brand new, girded with new vision, victory, and triumph?

who will look long enough
into her empty sockets
who will dare to see themselves
gazing there.

Whatever we give our time to will reward us. Zeal misdirected will eat you up, but zeal properly focused will energize, cultivate, and demonstrate the change you need. Are you cultivating a zeal for love rather than hatred? For compassion rather than complaining? For success rather than failure? Any attitude that does not welcome everyone is so toxic, it impacts all of us.

who will find the courage
to lift their legacy
out of the realm of the forgotten,
and speak the truth once again.

In Mark 4:14-15, Jesus teaches, "some people are like seed along the path, where the word is sown. As soon as they hear it, Satan comes and takes away the word that was sown in them." How do you ignore, undermine, marginalize, dispel, second-guess the Word in you? We all have the choice to stop listening to Absolute Good and instead start worshipping the voice of the inner critic. Some of us may hear the critic, who some call Satan, so distinctly that we view everything said to us through that lens. We diffuse the Word of God when we give credence to marginalization. What others say is not essential: our embrace of the power of spiritual law depends on what we tell ourselves.

not that we are looking for God,
but oh, that we
have found her.

Our goal is to move beyond the boundaries of fear and the confines of mediocrity and be courageous enough to do the work we are called to do, to use the energy that gives us the deep connection to divine source?

Stay in the upper room of prayer until you are guided by the Holy Spirit because through the zeal of your anointing, every portal, every channel, every stream of God's goodwill be open. You will no longer feel the shackles of limitation but will attain the remarkable and the miraculous. When you recognize the presence of God as your mind, body, and soul, you will make the right contribution to the loving energy of Spirit, which will always reveal what you need to know, when you need to know it.

I decree my legacy of zeal.

My Power is the God in Me

It's time to recognize our power.

I n the Book of Exodus, the 19th Chapter, it tells us that after the Israelites left Egypt, they came to the Desert of
Sinai, and Moses went up Mt. Sinai to God, where he was
given the Ten Commandments. The commandments are not
against us but are the most powerful tools for our success, meet-
ing us wherever we are in consciousness. The First
Commandment is "[y]ou shall have no other gods before me"
(Exodus 20:3). Moses says that if you center in God, if you recognize that God is the only power that there is, then through that
acceptance, you are delivered from slavery.

God's voice is not a loud voice outside of us, commanding what we must know. God's voice is the unlimited life within us, lifting us out of the realm of lack to express the dynamic energy of love that we are. This is the central truth of our being. The I AM is bigger than any condition in the flesh. The I AM is the Vortex of all creation recreating out of itself without limitation. The I AM is the energy of Spirit. There is no need to fight or condemn because that would be worshipping something and someone other than God.

My power is not pride in being a religion that is not in full acceptance of everyone, but in loving everyone from the power of the God in me. My power is the God in me, which knows that all things come together for our greatest good. The God in me rescues me from the river of abandonment, draws me out of the water of fear, allows me to leap—knowing that the net will appear, crowning me with victory before the race begins.

Embrace the God in you and lift up the power, peace, and joy of Moses' legacy on Mount Sinai to confess your belief in the I AM. Commit yourself to the greatness of all that you are. God never leaves you. God is always leading us out of the wilderness, into the full realization of God as us.

I decree my power is the God in me.

I am One with the Presence of God

It's time to put God first.

The Second Commandment says, "[y]ou shall not make for yourself an idol in the form of anything in heaven above or on the earth beneath, or in the waters below. You shall not bow down to them or worship them; for I, the LORD your God, am a jealous God, punishing the children for the sin of the fathers to the third and fourth generation of those who hate me, but showing love to a thousand [generations] of those who love me and keep my commandments" (Exodus 20:4-6). A lot is lost in the translations of the Bible. There is no direct copy and those who have studied the Bible in great detail, including in its original language, tell us that the real word is not jealous but "zealous." Our God is zealous, demanding our exclusive devotion. Does this mean that God will punish us?

No, it means that when we give our energy to people, circumstances, or situations other than the absolute good of Spirit, we deny our own power. There is no place where God is not. In the Bible, this is illustrated by the golden calves that were worshipped. Moses just stepped away for a short time, and when he returned, people were worshipping a golden calf (Exodus 32). How could they do something like that, we ask, and yet, we all do it. We worship golden calves every moment when we are not centered in Spirit, every time we lower our vibrations in fear.

When we panic, we give our energy to false idols. We cannot affirm that our wealth is from God, yet resent that we are not paid enough, worry about losing our job, or be doubtful that we will reap God's abundance in perfect divine order. We know inside, when we are worshipping a false idol, when we are worshipping the channel of God's good (the job, the gig, the person, the parent, the opportunity) rather than Spirit.

When we meditate, we lift ourselves above the attraction of false idols and connect to source unconsciously and consciously. We realize we are fed, lifted, strengthened, loved, and empowered by one source, and that source is the Spirit. Whenever we stop believing in Spirit, we worship false idols. When we believe in separation from our good, we miss the mark.

Sin comes from a Greek archery term, which simply means to miss the mark. God will never forsake us: the appearances of terror, of dis-ease, of losses have no power over us. No child is ever punished for the sins of their parents; we are not even punished for our own mistakes; we are punished BY them because we allow them to cut off the flow of God that is everywhere present.

Even the word God is an abstraction. We cannot just be in love with saying that we love God. If we say we love God and do not fully embrace the power and presence of God in every single aspect of who we are, in our thoughts, words, deeds, beliefs, then we are worshipping a false idol. We all have challenges that put us out of alignment with God's good, but our goal is to return from the far country into alignment with Spirit.

Practicing the presence of God maintains our connection. Practice the presence. Sit in meditation. Feel connected with God. The only thing you need to do is connect with the God in you and be forever in the flow of the unlimited good.

Do not bow down before any other power over your life because there is only one presence and one power. Know that when God's image becomes your image, when the within becomes the without, when you really center in the kingdom within, then you will be worshipping the true God.

I decree that I am the presence of God.

We are the Balm in Gilead

It's time to heal our heart.

In the Book of Luke, the First Chapter tells the story of Gabriel's blessing. After Zechariah and his wife Elizabeth had prayed and prayed for a child but had failed to give birth, after they had grown old and the possibility of ever having a child seemed impossible, they were visited by Gabriel. When there is something that we really want, God has a way of turning the impossible into the possible because nothing is *impossible* with God. And so it happened that while Zechariah, who was a priest, was attending to his ministerial duties, Gabriel came to bless him.

Now Zechariah apparently just saw a man, and we know if we study the Bible, sometimes that's how angels appear. They don't necessarily wear wings. They don't look a certain way, have a particular complexion—and definitely aren't limited to a particular ethnic group or religion. Angels come in all forms and shapes to help facilitate the goodness and the greatness of God. In fact, Hebrews 13:2 says do not forget to show hospitality to strangers, for by so doing, some people have shown hospitality to angels without knowing it.

Gabriel told Zechariah not to worry anymore because his prayers would be answered and that he would be blessed with a son, a son who will be filled with the Holy Spirit even before he was born.

But Zechariah didn't believe that. Zechariah questioned the good that was staring him right in the face. Our good comes in infinite channels, but we will never receive it unless we believe that we can. Zechariah was a priest, and he still didn't believe that he was entitled to God's Good. He asked Gabriel, "How can I be sure of this? I am an old man, and my wife is well along in years." However, Gabriel said, "I am Gabriel. I stand in the presence of God." *I am Gabriel. I stand in the presence of God.* I am not limited to what you see in the flesh. I carry with me blessings everywhere I go. I recognize that I am anointed. You may see the humanness of me but I beloved am gifted with the extraordinary love of Spirit.

He said to Zechariah, I have been sent to speak to you and tell you this good news. But here's the thing—because you did not believe me, I will silence you. You will remain mute. You will not be able to speak until your baby is born.

How often have we second-guessed God? There we have our blessing standing before us, and we don't want to believe that we are worthy. We don't want to trust that the infinite blessings of God always surround us and that his beloved Son, his beloved Gabriel is simply a witness, a reminder that God's source is inexhaustible.

Good medicine is the ability to heal by realizing that no past-present-future-time-space-body-limitation-lack-suffering has power over us. We are the power of perfect health and wholeness, power to be beyond a doubt, power to exhale with the presence of a Father-Mother-God that we know as the air we breathe and space that we take up.

Gabriel means *man of God; hero of God; presence of God; I AM power of God*. When we call on the angel Gabriel, that is when we center ourselves in the consciousness of Gabriel and summon God's blessings. We have to be open and receptive to them, or we will lose their immediate benefit. We are being taught that if we don't celebrate and trust the wonderful blessings of God, we only minimize, under-value, and depreciate their true worth.

When Gabriel came to Daniel in a vision, he didn't second-guess him. He was the one in the lion's den who got out when the lion's mouth was closed by an angel that many believe was Gabriel because when Daniel had to interpret a dream that was very difficult to interpret, Daniel heard a voice say, "Gabriel, tell this man the meaning of the vision." And Gabriel interpreted the dream. Daniel said on another occasion, while he was deeply in prayer, "Gabriel, the man I had seen in the earlier vision, came to me in swift flight and blessed me with insight and understanding."

Gabriel brings a special blessing regardless of who he touches, where he goes, and how he takes shape. Gabriel told Mary something that many of us remember and hold on to for ourselves. He said, "Do not be afraid, Mary for you have found favor with God." We all pray for favor with God, and Gabriel acknowledges that we have it. It is always present in our midst —with our birth into the realm of infinite possibilities. Gabriel is here in the Spirit but also in the flesh. Gabriel is the reminder to us of the infinite blessings that Spirit sends—sometimes in the guise of a dream come true, sometimes in the goodness of more happiness than we could ever imagine—sometimes with the birth of a baby.

I decree the birth of my good.

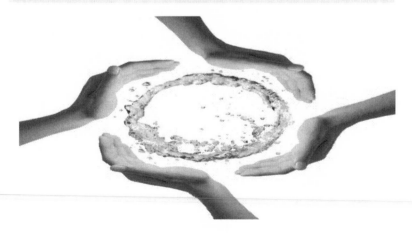

I Have a Superpower of Strength

It's time to be strong.

I n *Opening to Spirit*, Caroline Shola Arewa says that "we extend our roots down to the belly of the earth, she gives us strength to stand tall—and secure in her love, we make our ascent." Being grounded, drawing energy from the earth, is part of our faculty of strength. When we say, so and so "is the salt of the earth," we mean they are grounded. We say "stand on your own two feet"; "stand up for yourself,"; "stand your ground." Strength gives us discipline, responsibility, and service.

The story of David and Goliath illustrates strength. David, spiritual strength, had no armor or material protection (1 Samuel 17). David chose five smooth stones and put them in his shepherd's bag, and with his slingshot in his hand, David approached Goliath. Goliath was surprised to see that the only warrior who came forth was a little boy. David said to him, "[y]ou come against me with sword and spear and javelin, but I come against you in the name of the Lord Almighty, the God of the armies of Israel, whom you have defied. This day the Lord will hand you over to me, and I'll strike you down and cut off your head." David said "the battle is the Lord's, and He will give all of you into our hands, David and ran quickly toward the battle line to meet him (1 Samuel 17:46-50).

Goliath is that part of us divided from Source, and David is that part of us that rises with triumph, standing in the strength of Spirit. David said I do not have military training, but I know how to use what I have. David was saying, I do not have a spear, and I do not have a helmet. I have the earth under my feet and my slingshot. I have the whole armor of God. Reaching into his bag and taking out a stone, David slung it and struck Goliath on the forehead, and Goliath was defeated.

I have a superpower of strength that guides me when I am lost, protects me when I am vulnerable and lifts me when I thought I would never rise again. Spirit is the only strength I need, which always protects me with its might beyond what I could ever conceive.

I decree a superpower of strength.

"Something Amazing is Going to Come Out of This"

It's time to be our good.

I had a good fortune this week to hear the powerful story of Vernice "Flygirl" Armour, who went from beat cop to combat pilot in three years. Within months of earning her wings, she found herself flying over the deserts of Iraq, supporting the men and women on the ground. After serving two tours overseas, she became America's first African-American Female Combat Pilot. She tells the story of having to rescue her fellow Marines on the ground with only one missile left and 20-minutes of fuel and how she was called to push beyond her own fear of having little left to using what she did have to rescue those stranded. Months later, she was at the doctor's and met a Marine in line, who realized that she was the person who saved his life. But something else that she said stayed on my mind. She said my great-grandmother was a Unity minister at the same time as Johnnie Coleman. She said my great-grandmother always looked in the face of challenges and said, "something goooooood is gonna come out of this."

Her great-grandmother was Rev. Dr. Montee Falls from Memphis, Tennessee. Using Mark Hicks' Truth Unity website, www.truthunity.net, I learned that both her great grandmother Dr. Montee Falls, who was a successful educator at a high school, and her husband, Dr. Joseph Falls, who was the principal of the high school, and Master Bricklayer, were Unity Ministers and founded the "Unity Center of Memphis" with 12 members. Her grandmother, Rev. Mildred Falls Davis, became a licensed, ordained Unity minister in 1970. Her youngest daughter, Davine Davis, became an ordained Unity minister in 1988, and her middle daughter, Montee, also became a Unity Minister. So, within minutes after Vernice Armour spoke, I knew there were not one but five Unity ministers in her family, whose wisdom, education, brilliance, faith, and understanding of truth had endowed her with the power of good medicine.

Good medicine is knowing and fully embodying what Jesus said in Matthew 19:26, "with God, all things are possible." Great Grandmother Falls' legacy teaches us that something amazing will come out of whatever we are facing, that we all have permission to re-engage, and that the time to stop second-guessing Spirit is now.

Knowing that something good will come out of this pandemic helps us use our power to release the thoughts, hesitations, and fears that prevent us from moving forward. We can stop telling ourselves the old lies of "can't" when God says "we can."

We can tap into what Jesus called "good news." He says right in the scripture that our good does not end with his story, prophecy, or miracles but begins with the good medicine available to us all, the greater things we are summoned to do.

John teaches us that the Spirit of Truth will guide us in all things (John 16:13). All we must do is move out of its way. Good medicine is the good sense in us that believes beyond appearances that God can do for us as much as we allow God to do through us.

No matter what appears to be up against you now, know that something good will come out of it because that is what we are here to demonstrate.

I decree that something good is happening in my life right now.

I Let Go,
and I Let God

It's time to release.

The Fourth Commandment says, "[r]emember the Sabbath day by keeping it holy. Six days you shall labor and do all your work, but the seventh day is a Sabbath to the LORD your God. On it, you shall not do any work, neither you, nor your son or daughter, nor your manservant or maidservant, nor your animals, nor the alien within your gates. For in six days, the LORD made the heavens and the earth, the sea, and all that is in them, but he rested on the seventh day. Therefore, the LORD blessed the Sabbath day and made it holy" (Exodus 20:8-11). Sabbath means rest.

Genesis teaches that God created the universe in six cycles of activity, and on the seventh day, God rested. In every desire that we co-create, everything we desire to manifest, we must rest. We must trust the divine ethers, the quantum realm, the infinite source of nothing, nowhere, no place, and no time to do the requisite work, to facilitate the necessary connections, to make the divine appointments, to open the closed doors, to find the desired partner, to manifest the right resources, to tie the loose ends, to make a way out of no way, to do what we could never do for ourselves. We must let go and let God.

One of my favorite scriptures is Job 23:14 (NKJV), "For he performeth the thing that is appointed for me: and many such things are with him." Imagine what a pandemic Job experienced, a loss of everything. He said, "[o]n the left hand, where he doth work, but I cannot behold him: he hideth himself on the right hand, that I cannot see him. But he knoweth the way that I take: when he hath tried me, I shall come forth as gold" (Job 14:9-10). Job is saying I may not understand what is going on; I may not see the process, I may not see behind the scenes, but God is building, growing, pruning, shaping, improving, creating, performing, and completing what God appoints me to do. After I have done everything that I can do, I let go, and I let God.

Georgiana Tree West gives an analogy of our need to surrender to Spirit in her book, *Prosperity's Ten Commandments*. She says that when a farmer selects the seed, it is like us deciding what we want. When a farmer prepares the ground for planting, it is like us praying and acknowledging the one Source, the soil from which all of our good comes. We never create anything ourselves; God is always creating through us.

When we acknowledge the Source from which all good comes, then we are filled with the realization that it is inexhaustible. Planting the seed is when we accept our desires. We plant in the soil of the mind; we plant in the soil of the heart; we plant in the soil of our soul. Spirit is always blessing us with divine ideas, but we must accept them to plant them in our consciousness. Tending the weeds is when we cultivate our goals with faith; when we prune, shape, and co-create through meditation, visualizations, denials, and affirmations; when we join like-minded people to center in Spirit; when we journal; and when we meditate.

After the farmer has selected the seed, prepared the ground, planted the seed, and tended the garden, he waits. He cannot send roots down into the soil, put leaves on the stalks, or blossoms on the flowers. He must let go and know that Spirit is working to reveal the good that is constantly creating itself in the universal ethers. It would be ridiculous for him to stay up all night worrying about whether the seeds will grow.

It is always amazing that I can have what seems like a huge challenge in the evening and feel like I'm never going to get it done. But then, I go to sleep. I take a rest. I let go, and I let God. I surrender. And when I wake up, an amazing thing happens, the universe gives me exactly what I need in an instant. While I was resting, Spirit gave me what I needed. Every night is a Sabbath.

In Matthew 6:28, Jesus said, "Consider the lilies of the field, how they grow; they toil not, neither do they spin." Whether we are dealing with the seven days of a week cycle; the seven years of a life cycle; the 40 days of an accomplishment cycle; or the inexplicable period of a goal cycle, we must balance all that we do with rest, and in that consciousness of rest, surrender to Spirit.

We have all planted seeds during this pandemic, and one of its lessons is patience, how to let go and let God. The best for us is taking shape here and now, taking shape for generations to come, blessing us in the soil of the unseen. We can take our deepest desires to the altar of our souls and release them to be lifted into the absolute good of the kingdom of God. Only then do we enjoy the process of our growth, which is its greatest blessing.

We can prune and weed and water with more patient love, a more generous spirit, a more inspired attitude because we know that in our rest, there is not merely the stillness that comes with waiting, not merely light emerging from the dark tunnel of our impatience, not merely God performing all that we were called to do, but in our rest, there is always completion.

I decree that I let go, and I let God.

I Honor Spirit

It's time to know that I am Spirit.

The Fifth Commandment says, "[h]onor your father and your mother, so that you may live long in the land the LORD your God is giving you" (Exodus 20:12). It does not just say that we must respect and provide for our parents; that is the bare minimum. We must honor them. We must honor those who gave us our physical bodies, honor those who cared for us in our infancy, honor those who cared for us in our childhood, honor those who cared for us in our adolescence, honor those who cared for us as adults. Sometimes parents may have been abusive or continue to be abusive, so we must erect the necessary boundaries that we need for our own health, welfare, and well-being. But we must honor them, even if it means loving the divine in them from a distance. When we study the spirit of the scripture and not just its words, we realize that it is much deeper than honoring our human providers in the physical realm.

Kahlil Gibran, in *The Prophet*, says to parents, your children "come through you but not from you. And though they are with you yet, they belong not to you. You are the bows from which your children as living arrows are sent forth." In Matthew 23:9, Jesus says, "[d]o not call anyone on earth your father; for One is your Father, He who is in heaven." Jesus teaches us that we are spiritual beings clothed in physical bodies and that our parents are just the channels that Spirit uses to bring us into the world. Once again, the commandments teach us that the Source of all honor is God. It does not matter who birthed us; when the energy of the Holy Spirit is present, our parents are there.

Thich Nhat Hanh, a Buddhist monk whose parents were deceased, said in *Living Buddha, Living Christ*, "our mothers and fathers helped us come to be and, even now, they continue to give us life. Whenever I have difficulties, I ask for their support, and they always respond." Our ancestors are part of the infinite realm of Spirit. I honor the God that gave me a destiny in the irresistible vortex of my desires. I honor the Christ who died for me because in the second that my Savior died, I began. I honor the breath that the Holy Ghost breathed as me in the transformational moment of my spiritual liberation. I honor the Freedom that blessed me through the all-encompassing soul of my being. I honor my Mother and my Father, and in so doing, I honor all of who I AM.

Paramahansa Yogananda says that God becomes the Father to protect the child, the Mother to love the child unconditionally, and friends to help the soul without the limitations of familial instincts. It is God who becomes the food and breath and the life-sustaining functions. It is God who penetrates our understanding and awakens us to the duty and privilege to worship God templed in ourselves. It is God who loves us unconditionally. Do we really honor the greatest spiritual parent that there is, or do we just gladly accept whatever God gives and not even think about giving back through a consciousness that fully acknowledges the power of Spirit living and breathing as us?

I honor the all-knowing wisdom, all-giving love, all-flowing peace of God's heart beating as me, realizing I am in the heart of God. I honor the unlimited joy and calming grace that blesses me without ceasing. I honor the divine ideas that keep anointing me with fresh stories, new friends, untold strength, and cosmic energy. I honor the success, overflowing from the abundance of gifts in the irresistible vortex of my desires. I honor the Spirit moving through my life through a community and a deep connection of Oneness with each one of you. I honor the freedom that resurrects me through the all-encompassing soul of my being.

I decree my Mother-Father God is always honoring me.

I Breathe in the Power of God

It's time to connect with our power.

The Commandments are rules on a fundamental level—to govern our affairs in the physical but they are also how we open our mind and soul to be one with the absolute goodness of God, a goodness that is beyond shape or form, time or dimension but is in the quantum realm of supernatural power that is always available and expressing through us. When we find ourselves separating our thoughts, words, or deeds from the power and pure love that God expresses as us, the Commandments are the instructions that bring us back.

Metaphysically, Moses means salvation. Moses was not just drawn out of the water and saved as an infant, but he drew the

Israelites out of slavery and led them to freedom of the highest level of consciousness. Moses was an Egyptian Prince, royalty trained in the highest spiritual law. When he goes to the mountaintop, he does not merely do so in the physical realm; he ascends in consciousness. He climbs in his belief. He climbs in his faith, and when he does, he sees God. He is enlightened with divine principles, which we call the Ten Commandments. When you study them, you know that they did not just begin with the civilizations that co-created the scrolls canonized in the Bible; they are part of the many rules that evolved thousands of years before the Egyptians.

Together, the Commandments teach us that God expresses as us—every limb, every bone, every molecule, every vessel, every thought, every vision. MY POWER IS THE GOD IN ME. Don't give that power away to anyone or anything, or you find yourself worshipping a false idol. BE BLESSED NOT SCORNED by the Commandments, not as the rigid, impenetrable stones—hardened by time and misinterpretation but by the master light that breaks them into microscopic pieces that are digested by our souls and breathed in by our senses, that guide us and sustain us and carry us through our wilderness to the other side. This is the manna, the true bread that feeds and sustains us.

I decree I am blessed by the Commandments.

We are Between Each Moment

It's time to pause.

The physical body is organized patterns of energy and information, unified with everything in the quantum field. We all broadcast a distinct energy pattern or signature. In fact, everything material is always emitting specific patterns of energy. And this energy carries information. Our states of mind consciously or unconsciously change that signature on a moment-to-moment basis because we are more than just a physical body; we are consciousness.

When we become a quantum creator, we go from "cause and effect" to "causing an effect." We need to hold a clear intention of what we want but leave the "how" details to the unpredictable quantum field. Let it orchestrate an event in your life in a way that is just right for you. If you are going to expect anything, expect the unexpected. Surrender, trust, and let go of how the desired event will unfold.

The universe is over a trillion galaxies, hundreds of sextillion stars, and uncountable trillions of planets. There are particles, waves, and possibilities, and none of these things can be proven scientifically because the universe is constantly expanding itself. All can be defined as nothing because it cannot be proven scientifically. Most of it we cannot even see. Our experience of the physical world is really through our perception. We think that we are matter and substance, but we are really energy: pure consciousness. Some say that we are more Spirit than flesh because our concept of matter, shape, form, and body is what we see, what we sense, what we remember in our experiences. But sense is soul projecting itself into our individual expressions.

We have before us a canvas of absolute good. Our prayers are the brush that paints the canvas of our experience. Our souls are the spiritual energy that serves as the catalyst of our creation. But we do not paint with our hands; we paint with our hearts. This journey that we are on through this critical time of the spiritual evolution of this planet is about liberating ourselves to be masterful painters, co-creators of our experience. As Sojourner Truth said, "oh God, I didn't know you were so big."

I decree God is bigger than I can imagine.

I Cannot Destroy Absolute Good

It's time to uplift our greatness.

The Sixth Commandment says, "[t]hou shall not murder" (Exodus 20:13). When we read this commandment literally, we know that we are not supposed to murder, injure, attack, hurt another sentient being. But when we only read this superficially, we limit its meaning. The scripture is not merely talking about killing; it is talking about consciousness. We see ourselves as separate from other beings, but the truth is that we are one. We are Absolute Good, which is the pure life force of Spirit. We cannot destroy the goodness and greatness of anything or anyone.

Our greatest enemies are those of our own household—in other words, the thoughts of our own mind. We see Cain and Abel, two brothers, the sons of Adam and Eve, as separate, but spiritually, they are one: two parts of a whole. Cain was jealous, angry, bitter, and killed his brother Abel, who was kind, loving, and caring (Genesis 4:8). Cain symbolizes the material, the physical, and the flesh; his name means "possession." Abel means breath; he symbolizes the spiritual. We all have a physical and spiritual self that must be mastered.

The charge not to kill is deeper than just not murdering someone. Thou shall not kill also means that you will not undermine; you will not diminish; you will not ignore the lifeblood in yourself, which is the Spirit, the Power, the Kingdom, the Love within. To inflict violence upon someone else, you must feel some discord within. Thou shall not kill means we have to raise our consciousness to a higher level—above destruction, negativity, jealousy, fear, doubt, judgment—to do the good that we were called to do. We are all connected. When we attempt to destroy others, we destroy ourselves because we are all reflections of everyone else. We cannot destroy without destroying ourselves, and even in that attempt, we are still the eternal energy of God: a kingdom that always resides in us.

I decree the absolute good of Spirit loving as you and me.

I am True to Myself

It's time to be true to myself.

The Seventh Commandment says, "thou shall not commit adultery" (Exodus 20:14). From its Hebrew root, adultery means "a total or complete abandoning of one's principles." Jesus said, "If your right eye causes you to sin, gouge it out and throw it away. It is better for you to lose one part of your body than for your whole body to be thrown into hell. And if your right hand causes you to sin, cut it off and throw it away. It is better for you to lose one part of your body than for your whole body to go into hell" (Matthew 5: 29-30). In other words, if you are doing something inconsistent with your beliefs, stop doing it, which goes for relationships or anything else out of line with your integrity. I believe that another way of saying this commandment is "you shall not cheat yourself."

You shall not second-guess your infinite abilities to get everything that you ask for. You shall not do less than what God called you to do. You shall not interrupt the endless creative flow of good that God is pouring into your life.

You can be in a marriage committing adultery, even if you are faithful to your spouse in the physical sense. You are cheating your spouse and yourself if you do not want to be in the marriage, but you do not dare leave. The question is, are you living a life that is true to your soul?

This is a challenge for all of us. When people attempted to stone a woman accused of adultery, Jesus said, "Let he who has no sin cast the first stone." Everyone in the entire crowd left, and Jesus said to her, "go and sin no more" (John 8:7-11). Stop cheating yourself by being less than the powerful expression of the God within. If anyone gets in the way of your higher good and your greatest purpose, cast them away, and stop cheating yourself. Say to those mountains, move out of my way. Pull the log out of your own eye. Quit falling short of what you were called to do. Quit complaining about what you do not have. Give all your love, not a measured portion, but a cup running over. Go, and sin no more. Be nothing other than the fullness of your life. Stop cheating you, and be true to yourself.

I decree that I stop cheating myself.

Nothing or No One Can Block My Good

It's time to stop blocking our good.

We are on the Eighth Commandment, which is You shall not steal (Exodus 20:15). You will not steal. You cannot steal. Nothing can be stolen. Nothing can be taken from you. And you can't take anything that does not rightfully belong to you. No one and nothing in this universe can keep you from your greatest good. Nothing can interfere with the good that God is always blessing you with.

The Prophet Isaiah (49:1 NIV) said, "Before I was born the LORD called me; from my mother's womb, he has spoken my name." Jesus said that your Father knows what you need before you even ask. You cannot steal is not just about not snatching a purse or trying to take something that is not yours. That is easy to refrain from. What about realizing that you have gifts, talents, opportunities, divine order, deep wisdom, amazing grace, absolute good that is uniquely you?

Stay tapped into the higher vibration of your own good. Stealing is any type of deception, manipulation, cheating, lying, or fronting, and it all originates from the fear that we cannot demonstrate what we want. Our good comes from Spirit. I cannot steal, and no one can steal from me. I will not attempt to cajole, fool, mislead, or cheat the universe through manipulative misconduct because it always comes back to me. I cannot ridicule you, block you, or forbid you, or deny you from expressing who you are because the joy and love you express do not interfere with my greatest good.

I will let you finish your words without interruption. I will give you credit where credit is due. I will not try to control you because in freeing you, I liberate myself. I cannot steal because there is nothing that I do not already have through the infinite breath of God breathing me. We think "give" rather than "get." The thief denies the very force within which alone can help him, which is abundance. Stealing is like trying to steal the wave from an ocean, the wind from a breeze, the water from rain, or the love from God.

> *I decree that nothing and no one*
> *can take my good from me.*

I Walk in the Light

It's time to move in God's light.

The Ninth Commandment says, "You shall not give false testimony against your neighbor" (Exodus 20:16). When asked what the greatest commandment is, Jesus said, "[l]ove the Lord your God with all your heart and with all your soul and with all your mind" and says that the second greatest is "[l]ove your neighbor as yourself" (Matthew 22:36-40). Loving someone as ourselves deepens the meaning of this commandment. As 1 John 2:9-11 teaches us, "[h]e who loves his brother abides in the light, and in it, there is no cause for stumbling. But he who hates his brother is in the darkness and walks in the darkness, and does not know where he is going because the darkness has blinded his eyes."

How do we walk in the light? We walk in the light when we realize that we are one when we are, as Paul says in Hebrews 13:2-

3, so centered in loving our neighbors that we do not even "forget to entertain strangers, for by so doing some have unwittingly entertained angels." We walk in the light when we "[r]emember the prisoners as if chained with them—those who are mistreated—since [we] ourselves are in the body also." We walk in the light when we can breathe in the pain, affliction, and suffering of others and breathe out the love, light, and wholeness.

We walk in the light when we know that is it easy to refrain from bearing false witness in a moral sense, but that what really requires the work is to start by silencing our inner critic. Our inner critic is that negativity bias that we all have; that voice constantly says we are unworthy, not pretty enough, not young enough, not smart enough to inherit the kingdom. Our inner thoughts are our false witness.

In John 18:37, Jesus said, "[f]or this I was born, and for this I have come into the world, to bear witness to the truth." To bear witness to Truth is to know who we are and to express our true selves honestly. The Truth of us is the Christ in us. Here we are, locked into the mirror of our own being. We cannot hide by using our work because at some point, we have to look ourselves squarely in the face and be accountable—look into our own eyes, our own heart, the depths of our very being and ask whether we are really walking in the light.

What we say about others ultimately speaks volumes about ourselves. If I criticize you because of your accomplishments, then what speaks louder is my own sense of unworthiness. If I try to shame you because of something you did or did not do, I speak volumes about my own failure to walk in the light.

Shame is one of the lowest vibrations and most painful emotions that there are. Narcissists are known to undermine others by shaming them to their faces or behind their backs: telling them that they are not worthy because deep down inside, narcissists believe that they are not worthy.

We fat-shame people (too fat), skinny-shame them (too thin), age shame them (too young/too old), prosperity shame them (too rich), smart-shame them (oh you an egg head), relationship shame them (oh you too good for him). But what we say expresses our own consciousness, challenges, and frustrations about where we are.

We do not have time to throw shade when we walk in the light. We are too busy illuminating the kingdom within. I love the saying great minds talk about ideas, average minds talk about events, and small minds talk about people. If we are at the psychological stage of flight, fright, or fight, we cannot innovate with God's good in that state.

Negative criticism and gossip are poor self-regard, a subconscious attempt to cut another down so that we feel superior. But do we really? If we fail to walk in the light and rise above negative conjecture and criticism, we do not have the clarity to do what we are here to do. We should ask ourselves whether what we are saying needs to be said or learn from remaining silent. When we love our neighbors, we truly love ourselves. The angels that we desire to entertain are always around us, but we do not see them when we are stuck in the realm of shame and blame. This season of introspection gives us a rare opportunity to find the light that radiates as us, to meditate on it, embody it, be in it, and walk in it so that it fills every thought, every word, every deed, every communication, and every aspect of ourselves. How do we walk in the light? By making a commitment to ourselves to be the truth of inexhaustible supply, endless potential, and amazing grace that Spirit calls us to be.

I decree that I walk in the light today, and I shine my best.

I am One with the Presence of God.

It's time to practice the presence.

I was listening to Dr. Li Sumpter last night, an Afro-Futurist and Mythologist, a scholar in the re-creation of ourselves through the metaphysics of mythology. She spoke during a program given by Dr. David Ragland and the Truth Telling Project. One of the things that they shared is the importance to tell a new story that must also be a new prayer, a new narrative that provides for evolution and transcendence of the moment, and a new lens through which we can begin to re-envision and re-define ourselves.

As the Pulitzer Prize-winning Native American writer N. Scott Momaday wrote, "[w]e are what we imagine. Our very existence consists in our imagination of ourselves. Our best destiny is to imagine who and what and that we are. The greatest tragedy that can befall us is to go unimagined." It is through this lens that we embrace the Tenth Commandment: You shall not covet your neighbor's house; you shall not covet your neighbor's wife, or his man-servant, or his maidservant, or his ox, or his ass, or anything that is your neighbor's (Ex. 20:17).

If I seek first the Kingdom of God, I realize that there is no need to misappropriate or interfere with something belonging to someone else because the universe is always blessing us with what is for our highest good. There is a power in me that attracts what I need before I even ask, so I am not worried about what others have because I got it going on in me. If I covet what you have, I deny the power, purpose, and magnitude of my own life.

WE ARE SUPER-NATURAL, WITH THE ABILITY TO CO-CREATE WITH ENERGY THAT IS UNSEEN IN THE FLESH. WE CAN CO-CREATE THE TYPE OF EXPERIENCE THAT WE WANT TO HAVE BECAUSE THERE IS NO LIMIT TO WHAT THE UNIVERSE CAN DO FOR US.

I decree that I am one with a new story.

I Begin It

It's time to begin again.

W e must embrace the light within and realize the light beyond and the pure power of who we are. We must take responsibility for ourselves and not only claim our greatness but realize our truth. We cannot, must not, return to our old norms of fear, frustration, lack, doubt, complaining, worry, which enslaved us for so long.

This is the day that we stand at the portal of a new beginning. How do we begin it? What do we need to learn? This is our wake-up call. If we stay in a fixed mindset of complaining, we lower our immunity, heighten inflammation, enhance dis-ease.

1 Thessalonians 5: 16 says, "Rejoice always, pray continually, give thanks in all circumstances." Our gratitude mindset matters. A gratitude mindset is a growth mindset, which moves us

beyond our old norms, and allows us to change. One of our superpowers that supports a growth mindset is positive affirmations and visualizations. Matthew 7:7 says, "[a]sk and it will be given to you."

In one scientific study, where 350 adults volunteered to be exposed to the common cold, those who had the most positive emotions were less likely to develop a cold. Some of the same researchers wanted to investigate why happier people might be less susceptible to sickness, so they gave volunteers the hepatitis B vaccine in another study. Those who were more positive were nearly twice as likely to have a high antibody response to the vaccine. Positivity, the study found, helped the effectiveness of the vaccine.

Love is the only way to evoke the power of positivity. Love is the only way to begin again.

I decree that with love, I begin again.

My Superpowers
are Unlimited

It's time to acknowledge our superpowers.

I honor the mother who birthed the unique being called
me. I honor the Universal Ethers that formed every hair,
every molecule, every bone, every muscle, every fiber,
every divine vibration of I AM that I AM.

I honor the cosmic womb that delivered the light that shines
as us. I honor the Spirit that carried us into this reality of absolute good that we call life. I honor the Perfect Harmony that
called us from the endless bounty of this time-space continuum
before we were shaped in the womb. I honor the souls who came
before us and through whose legacy we were born, not simply
because we are, but because without them, we would never be.

I honor the God who gave me a destiny in the irresistible vortex of my desires. I honor the Ancestors—expressing through us the love of enlightened purpose and endless possibility. I honor Mary, her favor born in us, and her Son, the Christ, our Friend, who died because in the second that our Savior died, he lived in us.

I honor the breath that the Holy Ghost breathed as us in the transformational moment of our spiritual liberation. I honor my mother, and in so doing, I honor all of who I AM. I honor the mothers in our circle, expressing through each one of us. I uplift mothers as spiritual creators, divine beings, angels of light, miracles of strength, who do not only bring out the best in us but are the best in us. I am grateful for the mothers who are that part of us, who sacrifice to give and co-create with energy, resilience, commitment, and compassion to give birth to something greater than ourselves.

A mother is a deep wisdom in us that knows, really knows as much as God, and sees through all appearances of things and reaches beyond flesh to pull us back from waywardness to righteousness. A mother is that balance in us of carefulness and carefreeness, of resistance and release, of responsibility and blame, of praise and humility. My mother had five children, and I wanted to emulate her from a very early age, so I sat on the porch with about five dolls lined up under my care and protection because I appreciated the sacred act of mothering and the love that she gave me.

Thich Nhat Hanh says that our mothers are so profoundly connected to us that they continue to nurture us even when they have left the fleshly realm, that they never stop giving us life, that we can always call on their support. When someone sings, "sometimes I feel like a motherless child," we feel their pain because we know that those words mean they have lost spiritual grounding. They can no longer see the spiritual ancestors who continue to give birth to us, love, protect, and heal us.

Our mothers are reservoirs from which the continuous stream of good constantly flows into our lives, a stream that has nothing to do with money or bank accounts—but flows endlessly from inexhaustible supply. Our mothers are all-knowing wisdom, all-giving love, all-flowing peace constantly enriching us, cleansing our hearts, healing our souls. Our mothers are complete faith, unlimited joy, and calming grace that blesses us with a life so wonderful that we have never even dared to imagine it.

Our mothers are divine ideas that keep anointing us with fresh stories and new friends, and untold strength and cosmic energy. Our mothers are the success, overflowing from the abundance of gifts in the irresistible vortex of our desires. Our mothers move through our lives through a community called prayer and a deep connection of Oneness within each one of us. Our mothers are the freedom that resurrects us through the all-encompassing souls of our being.

Our mothers are the prayers that are always answered, always blessing us, regardless of the external world. We can stand on the shoulders of our mothers and be lifted in the buoyancy of their grace. We ride the waves of their magnificence beyond the pandemic through a new portal of victory. Our mothers nurture and heal, bless and protect, stir and fulfill, create and innovate. Mothers guide and give, find ways out of no ways, move beyond the mountain, part the seas, and inspire the manifestation of even greater things.

I decree celebration of the mother in me.

I Have a Superpower of Faith

It's time to believe.

Prayer is not the asking but realizing God's full power and presence, realizing that we are spiritual beings having a human experience. Without faith, our belief in things unseen, we cannot connect with any of these teachings. Peter, who had faith that Jesus was the Messiah, represents our power to believe in the unseen. Faith quickens our spiritual understanding: our power to see beyond the physical to the deeper realm of dreams, visions, symbols, connection, prophecy, revelation, and the realization that surpasses all that we see in the flesh—beyond appearances, as Jesus says judge, not by appearances but judge by righteous judgment (John 7:24). With faith, we can rise above the appearances of any circumstance, realizing that the universe conspires to help us manifest our good. Often, despite our failure to tap into faith, we are blessed.

My favorite story that illustrates the power of faith is the story of Joseph. His life began as a pandemic when his brothers, through their jealousy of the coat his father gave him and many other things, sold him into slavery, and yet he had the extraordinary vision to see beyond his circumstances, to interpret dreams to prophesy, to envision. He was literally ditched by his brothers, falsely accused, and imprisoned, yet he rose to become one of the most powerful men of Egypt, which represents the material world. And even when the day comes and he sees his brothers face to face, who does not even know who he is at first, his brothers have nothing—and he doesn't seek revenge but tells them in Genesis 50:20, don't worry, you meant it for evil, but God meant it for good.

Faith orders us to quit standing on the periphery of our good and step into the power that we are. Allow your blessings to take shape. Have faith that there is a superpower in you that is greater than what is in the world. Have faith that you can transform everything in your midst into a new creation, and nothing and no one can stop you.

I decree that
all good will be restored.

I Have a Superpower of Metta

It's time to spread metta.

Metta means lovingkindness. Metta or loving-kindness helps us see life and experience it through a lens of love—connection, fullness, kindness, warmth. Whatever we give our attention to will grow. If we give our attention to hate, fear, animosity, doubt—it will grow. But if we give it to generosity, patience, kindness, and love—that will grow. It is like taking a path over ground that may be thick and difficult to navigate at first, but the more you take it, the more you go down the path—the easier it becomes, so we want to be on the right path, carving deeper into the energy and awareness of metta.

Our superpower of metta grows and enhances and helps us more when we become more aware of it and invite ourselves to widen our hearts through kindness. Finding this state of awareness with metta, with lovingkindness, is learning to be with our best selves. In John 14:2, Jesus said, "In My Father's house are many mansions; if it were not so, I would have told you. I go to prepare a place for you." The Father's house is where we are grounded in goodness, where we realize the willingness to be fully present to who we are and allow life to touch us.

Our metta is so strong we do not have to be together. But we still see each other, we feel our spirits connect with our souls—across the appearances of boundaries, and we know we are one. The only way we will emerge entirely from these spaces of protection, these healing restorative wombs of spirit—the only way we will emerge from these cocoons of metta that we sit and ponder in each day is by changing our hearts—is by realizing that we are in the hearts of God, is by sitting in the power of metta until it seeps through every muscle and penetrates our bones. We have to wake up, not merely to "be woke" but to know that the most important way to emerge is through the heart of God, through the infinite power of metta; only then will our wings lift us from this experience and allow us to soar in a new way.

I decree that I send metta
throughout the world.

I Have a Superpower of Present Moment

It's time to know the present moment.

L ovingkindness is the practice of being with the present moment, which is the key to our resilience and well-being. It is breathing in the present with clarity and focus and returning to it when our mind wanders when we get off track: that is the practice of meditation. It is not just with the present moment without interruption because we will be interrupted. The heart of the practice, which is why it is called practice—is being able to shift, pivot, return to where we need to be, which is with the present moment.

We ask ourselves, where is God? God is in the present moment. God is between the spaces where we breathe, in the pause when we know, and in the goal that we reach. The good news is that our human ability to conceive God doesn't matter because God is everywhere that we are. God is the present moment, and when we go into the silence, we can sit with peace, simply connecting with each breath of God that we pause to appreciate.

The present moment allows us to open spaces to heal, to stretch beyond knowing to unknowing, to be curious, to release the appearance of pain and suffering. Just because God is always something better in store does not mean that we don't hurt. But the present moment alleviates our pain because, in those instances, we know that we are healed.

We are the container of lovingkindness, which can be poured into our day without limit. Lovingkindness has no bottom; it doesn't empty after continued use; it gets fuller. In each present moment, we have the power to speak lovingkindness and feel the vibration of its words echo back.

Lovingkindness is the bridge to realizing we are one. Lovingkindness is the path of righteous judgment that Jesus spoke of when he said judge, not by appearances. Lovingkindness is the way, the truth, and the light when we expand beyond wanting to giving and condemning to appreciating. Lovingkindness is the grace that blesses us each day.

I decree the present moment of lovingkindness.

I Have a Superpower of Prayer

It's time to pray from the heart of God.

We have a superpower of prayer. When we speak, think, see, hear, send, breathe our prayers into the inexhaustible supply of the universe, we change the world. We can pray for ourselves, pray for others, pray for the planet. Nothing limits us, except for our own lack of imagination. We can pray boldly and without ceasing. We can also go to that place of silence, to that secret place. We can go within, sit in the moment, reconnect with the now, and just listen.

Prayer is our connection with the higher energy of Source— what I explained at the beginning of our journey as the quantum realm, endless energy, or waves of possibilities that we shape and form with desire. We can speak prayer through denials: nothing and no one can keep our good from us. We can also speak prayers through affirmations: we are success. We can also accept the answers to our prayers with gratitude, even before we ask.

The power of prayer is not in asking but in knowing. This is not something to argue about with other faiths. Our prayers are for connecting with the realization of God for ourselves. For me, that means everywhere, everyone, and everything present. Pray from the vast realm of nothing that penetrates everything. Pray from the universes and galaxies that cannot be accounted for because they are infinite.

In the heart of God, I do not have to ask for anything. All I must do is be still and know.

Here I am, in a prayer that needs nothing.

Here I am, knowing that I have what I need *before I even ask.*

Here I am, with prayers flowing around me like endless streams of blessings, pouring enough miracles to cover every want, desire, or need.

I decree that I am a prayer that needs nothing.

I Have a Superpower of Wisdom

It's time to embody wisdom.

W isdom is not book smarts, degrees, or intellect; wisdom is the discernment that comes from the supernatural, the Christ consciousness, the Holy Spirit, the Divine Mind: it knows beyond knowledge, seeing beyond the unseen, trusting in the Universe, co-creating with the quantum realm to do what we have to do without even being sure of why we're doing it. When we awaken to the reality of our being, we see, we trust, we rely on the light within, which is the truth: the embrace, the embodiment of our power of wisdom.

When this connection with wisdom is made, we find ourselves able to discern, judge, and decide. We know that the gentle nudge, the small still voice, the catalyst, the epiphany, the truth is there to steer us in the right direction. We can feel what to do and say and know in our gut, heart, bones, aura, vibration, frequency, signs that serve as our navigational system, our internal alarm, our wake-up call—to let us know how to proceed. We call that gut feeling—discernment; we call it mother wit; we call it the power of judgment. The best way to cultivate it is to be silent, so we can turn off the outside noise.

Think of your thoughts as a constant barrage of noise—like engines and sirens and blasts. Only if you quiet the noise can you observe the listener. The practice of connecting with self is connecting with Spirit. We need to make that connection as often as possible. I get up at 4 AM because I am more tuned into Spirit then. I write better; create better; listen better as it is quiet around me and in my soul. True wisdom is not determined by how much you think you know but by how comfortable you are in not knowing but trusting in Spirit.

Wisdom is emotional intelligence: self-awareness, self-regulation, empathy, humility, and pro-social behavior. People who have the best judgment are more concerned with being present for others and less concerned with impressing them; more concerned with learning more than lingering on the little they think they know. Wisdom is being able to say I do not know; I need help.

An African proverb says, the "wise aim at boundaries beyond the present; [and] by their struggle they transcend the circle of their beginning." Langston Hughes said, "I've known rivers: I've known rivers ancient as the world and older than the human blood in human veins. My soul has grown deep like the rivers."

Spirit gives us the discernment, the wisdom, the judgment that we need, which may be beyond human comprehension. I realize that I am blessed by what may appear to others as misfortune. I am blessed by what may appear to others as sickness. I am blessed by what may appear to others as lack. I call it all good, and by so doing, I send power into the spiritual ethers that attract even more thoughts of joy, contentment, and success.

James 1:5 says if any of you lacks wisdom, you should ask God, who gives generously to all without finding fault, and it will be given to him. The knowledge that we need is always in our midst. As Robert Fulghum says, "[w]isdom was not at the top of the graduate school mountain, but there in the sandbox in the nursery school. These are the things I learned: Share everything. Play fair. Don't hit people. Put things back where you found them. Clean up your own mess. Don't take things that aren't yours. Say you're sorry when you hurt somebody. When you go out in the world, watch for traffic, hold hands, and stick together. Be aware of wonder. Everything you need to know is there somewhere."

One of the best illustrations of this is the nomadic tribe Wayne Dwyer talks about in *Inspiration*. This tribe lived on the water off the coast of Thailand. They historically passed down the wisdom of *tsunamis* through generations and constantly stayed connected to Spirit. So, when one of them noticed a shifting pattern in the water in 2004, they alerted everyone to move to higher ground. There were no huge egos involved; no one was jockeying to give the last word; everyone without exception trusted his judgment. They left their villages and their boats and moved to higher land, and they all watched as the water did what they knew what it was about to do. The *tsunami* destroyed every boat and every home, yet the entire tribe was safe.

I decree a superpower of wisdom.

I have a Superpower of Dominion

It's time to remember we have dominion.

The Psalmist says in the 8th Psalm, Verses 8-6, that we are "endowed with dominion over all things." We are mightier than the world than all that takes place around us. We are more than mere creatures. We are the pure creative power of Spirit, made in its image and likeness, both flesh and divine, bigger than our physical form because we are part of the whole being of God, stronger than our human frailty because we are the strength of our Mother-Father-Everything-Almighty-Everywhere God. Our dominion, our ability to rule, starts with us.

We are all brilliant geniuses with the power to mold, shape, and be co-creators.

Dominion is also defined as supreme authority and absolute ownership. We are here as separate beings in the flesh and as intricate parts of a powerful whole. Break the cycles of weakness of anything less than the power of God radiating as us. Here and now, reclaim the power that we are and the dominion that we share. Why should we limit ourselves to standing on the shoulders of our ancestors when we can fly! We can soar beyond asking to the fullness of the Spirit.

What do you want to co-create from this unlimited birthright of dominion? What was your soul summoned to do before you were shaped in the womb? Will you be, as Jesus says, about your Father's business? Will you dislodge yourself from getting stuck in the appearances of imperfections, the half-truths, or the whole lies of being less than so that you surrender to the universe, to the unlimited possibility of living of your soul? Through our deepest desires, through those things that we love to do, through what we are most passionate about doing, through what makes us whole, through what helps rather than harms, we use our dominion over all that is less than Spirit to help God's good take shape.

I decree dominion over all things.

I Have a Superpower of Overcoming

It's time to overcome.

In John 16:33, Jesus said, "[i]n this world, you will have tribulation. But take heart! I have overcome the world." The law of overcoming means discerning what we need to keep in our lives and what we need to release. When a group of people who had succeeded in their dreams was examined, one of the things they had in common is their ability to overcome whatever they faced: their ability to break away from the crowd, ignore conventional wisdom, and move forward regardless of risks. The only thing that I remember from Finance 101 at Howard University is that the only risk-free investment is a guaranteed loss. Without risk, you always lose; but it is at least possible to succeed if you take a risk.

Overcoming requires us to do what Jesus said in Matthew 6:24 to decide whom we will serve. Jesus said, "[n]o one can serve two masters." Either we serve Spirit, or we serve flesh. Serving Spirit means lifting our consciousness above the world to recognize it and fulfill our calling to change it, but do not worship the flesh. Serving Spirit means tapping the powers of the spiritual gifts that guide us. Overcoming means getting over ourselves—moving beyond bad habits, beyond the inner critic, beyond the urge to believe that we are not worthy and instead co-create with the universe so that the good everywhere present can appear.

Overcoming is not for the faint of heart. We can turn our stumbling blocks into stepping-stones. We can use losses to make ourselves stronger. We can allow criticism to ignite our persistence. We can push through our own impatience past what no longer serves us to attain our goals. When we overcome flesh for Spirit and remain committed to our calling, God blesses us— the universe conspires to give us something better than we could ever imagine.

We shall overcome, not just one day but here and now.

I decree an overcoming spirit.

I Have a Superpower of Ownership

It's time to own our power.

S spiritual ownership is not about owning material things. Our choices are shaped by our willingness and desire to own our relationship with the world. In 2 Corinthians 1, Verses 21-22, Paul tells the Corinthians, God anointed us, set his seal of ownership on us, and put his Spirit in our hearts as a deposit, guaranteeing what is to come. But this infinite power of absolute good takes cues, direction, guidance from us. God guarantees help, but how God helps us depends on what we need. God hears the still small voice in us, the doubt, that crazy inner critic—uttering one thing when we really want to experience the exact opposite.

We can align ourselves with the pure power that we are. Are you owning the gifts, talents, abilities, infinite possibilities you are, or telling yourself that you are not worthy and settling for something less?

Our anointings shine from our souls—from God expressing as us. 2 Corinthians 1:20-22 says we are all anointed. The question is—do we own up to our anointing? The scripture also says God has put his Spirit in our hearts as a deposit. When we have clarity of what we are here to do, we can better align with our true purpose and calling to be disciplined, study, do the work, and take ownership of what we are here to do.

Ownership requires that we be honest with ourselves about using whatever we have available to accomplish what we must do, realizing Spirit will guarantee the outcome. In Chapter 1 Verse 5, Jeremiah says that before I formed you in the womb, I knew you; before you were born, I set you apart. The question is whether you are willing to own up to what is already guaranteed. Yes, I will own my purpose, and here is the law—if I own the work that I am anointed to do, God will guarantee my success.

I decree my destiny.

I Have a Superpower of Oneness

It's time to know we are one with God.

I n his letters, Paul begged the Philippians to "make his joy complete by being like-minded, having the same love, being one in spirit" (Philippians 2:2 NIV). We are one in Spirit, and through this oneness, we evolve even more effortlessly with the synergy, synchronization, and blessings of God. Through his radical change, Saul became Paul and made available to us a oneness with Christ consciousness that continues to transform. Paul said, in Acts 17:28, "[f]or in him, we live and move and have our being. As some of your own poets have said, '[w]e are his offspring.'" We are one.

There is no separation between all that God is and all that we are. In John 10:30, Jesus says, "I and the Father are one." In John 17:11, he said, "Holy Father, protect them by the power of your name, the name you gave me, so that they may be one as we are one." And watch this; in John 17:20-21, Jesus says, "I pray also for those who will believe in me through their message, that all of them may be one, Father, just as you are in me and I am in you."

I was talking to a friend of mine last night because another friend just died. My friend said that she had a dream the night before, and in the dream, she was at her funeral. When we are one with Spirit, what we need to know will be revealed. Marja de Vries says in her book, *The Whole Elephant Revealed*, "[b]ecause all the wisdom traditions see the beginning of everything as Oneness, the first universal law, the first principle, is the Law of Oneness. The Law of Oneness states that everything that exists emanates from one and the same Oneness of Source."

We are One because we share the breath of Spirit. We share the Divine Mind; we share Infinite Wisdom. We cannot be selfish about something that does not belong exclusively to us. Oneness assures all of us of the pure potential of Spirit. The better we know our own nature, the closer we come to actualizing the greatest things we are here to do.

I decree our oneness.

I Have a Superpower of Order

It's time to be in perfect, divine order.

I want to focus on order today, but not the kind of order that is linear—where everything is done step by step—in what appears to be a neat physical sequence, falling in line in a way that aligns with our suggested order of what should happen. Order is deeper than what we see and want and try to control. The order of the universe is not as readily apparent because we often do not see the alignment of God working together for our good in the physical realm. In the quantum realm, there are many different outcomes, which physicists say are happening simultaneously, without beginning, middle, or end. Scientists say that order is actually timeless, beyond past, present, and future. I believe that order is aligned with our greatest good.

This is the kind of order that Job teaches us about in Job 23:14, where Job—whose life appeared to be everything but organized said: "God performs the thing that God appoints me to do." Sometimes we get caught up in our own agendas, but Spirit directs us in the flow of God's order. When we trust God's plan and purpose, expressing through the fulfillment of God's greatest desires calling us, we realize the divine order and ease of good flowing in everything around us.

The Psalmist says (Psalm 138:8)(NKJV), "[t]he Lord will perfect that which concernth me." Joseph's brothers did not recognize him at first, and when they did, they were terrified. But Joseph told them that even though they meant him evil, God meant him good. Jesus talks about order when he reminds us in Matthew 9:37 that "[t]he harvest truly is plentiful, but the laborers are few." As the Psalmist says in Psalm 37:23, "[t]he steps of a good man are ordered by the Lord." Order is trusting that the universe will align everything we need when we need it for our greater good. We better align ourselves with divine order when we take purposeful pauses throughout the day, which means not getting on the phone, searching our email, or watching Netflix, but just pausing and breathing in our connection with God.

I decree that my life is in perfect divine order.

I Have a Superpower of Soul

It's time to connect with our soul.

The soul is the highest form of the self. The presence of the soul brings the presence of God. Brown Landone wrote a book called *Soul Catalysts*, which says, "the soul is not in your body, but . . . your body is in your soul, and hence your body is but the focal point of your soul in expression." The soul is where we center ourselves, the kingdom in which we live, move, and are the pure power of absolute good. When we connect with the divine energy that we call the soul, we feel the unconditional love that is always blessing, guiding us, favoring, and anointing us beyond time, space, or body.

In the timelessness of the soul, we can sit in the love and the light of not worrying about or needing anything, simply being one with God. In the soul, we know that everything we desire is already taken care of before we even breathe in this powerful connection with all that Spirit is. If you have a worry or a concern, just allow yourself to carry that to the soul, unlimited in the absolute good of Spirit, and as soon as you surrender whatever the burden is, you will know that it is blessing you beyond appearances. You will know that whatever you need in that circumstance is already taken care of.

Just feel the joy of your connection with your soul radiating with pure vibrations into our circle of prayer, and see our circle fully expanding love in the light of divine connection. This incredible circle of our souls blesses us and uplifts us as the love, light, and power that we are, spreading the energy of our circle throughout our communities, in cities, states, countries, and throughout the planet. The power of the soul is not merely being alone but is in its connection to all that is. Souls connect with all other souls, aligned with the love and light of Spirit.

Feel the joy of knowing your soul and realizing that it is always blessing you, uplifting your authenticity, embodying you with perfect health and wholeness, opening your heart, filling you with the pure love of all that needs to be at the end of a prayer.

I decree the power of my soul.

I Have a Superpower of Love

It's time to love like nothing else.

G od is an energy out of which we are formed, an energy that we have come to call "love." The problem is that we have forgotten the very essence out of which we were created. We have forgotten our true roots, that they are not of a place or a people but that they are the energy of Love. We are not separate from the infinite force and inexhaustible source of creative energy that called us into being. Love emanates from every pore, divine vibration, and Spirit-infused idea that gives shape to us. When we embrace the powerful energy of all that Love is and allow ourselves to be its co-creative channel of good, it gives us all that we need, want, and desire.

Love is much bigger than who we are in the flesh.

Pure love has nothing to do with romance.

In *The Prospering Power of Love*, Catherine Ponder says, "[y]ou do not have to search outside yourself for love. You can begin releasing it from within outward, through your thoughts, words, actions, and affirmative prayers. As you do, you will experience the successful power of love in all its fullness as its works through people, situations, and conditions that concern you."

If you shine your light as Love, the love you seek CANNOT be withheld from you. If someone is bothering you, send love their way and watch what happens. If you have an injury or an ailment, send love your way and watch what happens. If you desire, dream, or set goals, keep sending love their way and watch what happens. If you want a divine partner, send love to the universe, and the right person will manifest for you.

Love cannot withhold from you what you need. Withholding defies the very nature of Love; it cannot happen. The good that you seek through the power of Love will always be radiated back to you.

The Bible can be written in one word: LOVE.

If we all loved completely and unconditionally, we would never have to read, study, or try to understand the stories of the Bible.

Samahria Lyte Kaufman, in *Love Wins*, tells the story of her son Raun who was diagnosed as autistic at 18 months old. After six months, he began to be completely disconnected from people. But instead of judging him, she just decided to love him and began to work with him 12 hours a day, seven days a week, for three and a half years. During that time, Raun was mute and unresponsive. But because of the love that she gave him, not only did he get better, Raun graduated from Brown University with a degree in biomedical ethics. Kaufman offers some pearls of wisdom for tapping our faculty of love. She says that we must love in the fullest way possible, without worrying whether we will get anything back.

How do we love enough to win the challenge of whatever we are confronted with? We move beyond doubt, worry, fear, and discomfort and tune into ourselves. What are we feeling and why? What is the true source of our discomfort? Are they the source of an old story, unhealed wounds, trauma suffered by our ancestors, fear of the unknown? Can we evaluate our suffering and face it with love and compassion or ourselves? Can we release whatever we are feeling with love?

I love healing circles because they enable us to hold space and give us the strength to move through harm by facing, acknowledging, processing, and letting go. Perhaps healing circles should be called circles of love. Every challenge is an opportunity to show love, a decision that blesses us.

During a metta retreat, Spirit gave me a new mantra because the general lovingkindness mantra has never resonated with me. Instead, I thought, "I am light. I am love. I am whole. I am grace."

I am light. I am pure energy that is all presence, radiating everywhere until it is nowhere, penetrating all things until it is nothing, pouring into everyone until it is no one.

I am love. I am the gift of absolute good, pouring myself into streams of endless good so that I am a blessing to all beings.

I am whole. I am the connection we all share: the perfect health and wholeness of all that Spirit is, which connects us beyond the physical and the flesh and unites us in the joy of life.

I am grace. Grace is above cause and effect. Grace is forgiveness, the release of all suffering. Grace is the full embrace of God with the full acceptance that all that God is, I am.

I decree I am love, light, and grace.

I Have a Superpower of Power

It's time to uplift our power of power.

I realized the magnitude of power after I passed out on the subway one day. I was in my twenties and was coming home from work and was not feeling good. After getting off the A Train and making it onto the platform before transferring to the F Train, I passed out. After I fainted on the subway, the thought of going back into the subway made me anxious, so I avoided it. I took the bus instead. But as I rode the bus to work one day, I read a book by William Warch called *Your Twelve Gifts From God*. The chapter on "Power" changed my life.

A power called "Power" may seem redundant, but it is not. The superpower of power is our ability to choose to experience life in a new way. Regardless of what is in the world, we have the power to choose how we will respond to it. Our power is only limited by our beliefs. We can choose to be well, choose to succeed, choose to be wealthy, choose to be strong, choose to tap wisdom, choose to find the wherewithal to re-invent ourselves.

After Jesus was resurrected, he said (Acts 1:8), "you will receive power when the Holy Spirit comes upon you." The Bible does not say that if you want power, ask God for it. Jesus said, "you will receive power [when you are open and receptive to Absolute Good] when the Holy Spirit comes upon you." Has the Holy Spirit come upon you?

2 Timothy 1:7 says that "God did not give us a spirit of timidity or fear, but a spirit of power." The sooner we recognize our power, the sooner we accomplish our goals, the sooner we evolve and grow into a completely new existence.

We do not merely speak truth to power; we listen with power. True listening is extra-sensory. We say that we communicate with the spiritual energy surrounding us, with Absolute Good shaping us. With all of the violence in the world, including racism and hatred, we all need to tap our power to be better. Like a light switch, we can change our mindsets and click on the powers in our souls to change the world. But we need to start with ourselves.

I decree the superpower of power in me.

I Have a Superpower of Creativity

It's time to co-create in Spirit.

Our Creative Power has several dimensions. We have the power to envision, to imagine, to be open and receptive to God's Divine Ideas. The other aspect of our Creative Power lies in our belief in the manifestation of our good. Creativity is that step beyond the precipice where we trust the unknown. Our power to create is when we freely move beyond the edge of what we know in the flesh to trust what God can do through us in the Spirit.

Spirit is the co-creative force of every breath that we breathe and the energy that we expel. When we forget that we are divine ideas; when we just look at what we can do in the flesh; when we stop tapping into and turning on the infinite power of the universe, we cannot do what we are here to do. The journey is not about us; it is about the creative power of Spirit expressing as us. When we trust fully and completely in Divine Mind, without our second-guessing, we stop limiting what we can do in the flesh and start creating through the dreams that have summoned us to this existence.

We see, imagine, and create by trusting in the Universe, by saying yes, by going beyond our edges into the larger creative energy of the universe. Only when we move beyond our edges by facing who we really are and our experiences do we fulfill our desire to create. When we allow the creative consciousness of Spirit to lead us, we realize that opportunities are infinite. When we move beyond our fears, we see that our greater good is always here.

I decree that I move beyond fear
and manifest endless opportunity.

I Have a Superpower
of Understanding

*It's time to understand the benefits
of the Kingdom.*

The Zen teacher Edward Brown teaches us about under-standing in *The Tassajara Bread Book*. He says that when he first started cooking at Tassajara, he could not get his biscuits to come out the way they were supposed to. The problem was that he grew up thinking perfect biscuits had to be like the ones made by Pillsbury. But one day, he finally tasted his biscuits without comparing them to some previously hidden standard and realized just how good they were. We try to look good rather than to understand the uniqueness of our own rec-ipe.

Our challenges are the things that reveal our character, our values, our purpose, as well as our understanding. But we stand on the shoulders of what we have endured. We stand on the power of the spiritual enlightenment that we receive.

In the late '80s, there were several cases about babies dropped out of windows. But the babies did not die. The babies broke their falls because they grabbed curtains or tree branches to break their falls. It can be said that Spirit caught them. Spirit was standing under them. No matter who we are or where we fall, Spirit stands under us as our constant, present source of reinforcement.

As we grow older, our understanding becomes even more profound. If we pay attention, our inner guidance tells us where to go and what to do and not forget certain things. The power within us that guides our every move is understanding. Spirit does not have to shout. If we are open and receptive, Spirit breaks our fall, saves us, gives us life, makes safe and easier our path, reveals what we must do, provides us with force beyond our own understanding. As my favorite poet, the late Lucille Clifton, says in *The Book of Light*, "you are beyond even your own understanding."

God stands under all things and blesses us with a superpower of enlightenment.

I decree that everything I need to know
is being revealed to me.

I Have a Superpower of Will

It's time to exercise the will of God.

In John 5:30, Jesus says, "I seek not mine own will, but the will of the Father which hath sent me." There's a reason for not listening to our own will. If we seek, abide by, or obey our own will rather than God's will, we are apt to get it twisted. If we just do what we want to do in the flesh, we forget what we were called to do in the Spirit. Our superpower of will works in conjunction with our superpower of understanding. No matter how well we understand spiritual laws, our intellectual knowledge does not matter if we are unwilling to adhere to them. We are all guilty of not being obedient enough to listen, or even when we do listen, of not being willing to do what we must do. But when I am about my Father's business, I stop misdirecting my energy and seize each moment to be responsive to Spirit's call.

We sit at the threshold of the pandemic, where God is saying here is a new canvas, here is a new opportunity, here is a new stretch, here is a space of rest and recreation. I use this opportunity to continue better habits, a sounder disposition, and finish those projects long awaiting my attention. We are at the precipice of a shift in nature, a shift in science, a shift in connection, a shift in love, a shift in how we treat our bodies, minds, and souls because the Universe will not let us be who we used to be. As we try to determine what course to take, we should honor the presence of Spirit standing under all things, with a knowledge that defies the physical realm. We just need to be willing to hear and obey its guidance.

We need to let go of who we used to be and put on a new self. We should exercise the will to stop giving our energy to others, stop hiding behind bad habits and relationships, stop comparing, stop defining ourselves by somebody else's standard, stop believing that we are anything less than the image and likeness of our creator.

In the morning, when I rise, I tap the kingdom of God in which I dwell; when I am willing to be open, receptive, and willing to share the Word that God gives me, I am blessed. In the flesh, there is no way, but through the Spirit emerges a way out of no way. I just need to be willing to do the work, willing to cultivate and grow the habits that best serve my health.

This is the time to cleanse the toxins from our lives. We can taste the freedom of a new day, but we must do the work that Spirit guides us to do. Sometimes we are so wrapped up in the anxiety of the future, we are not even willing to embrace the power of the present moment. We may feel like we are weak, incompetent, or floundering. We may see nothing but chaos, confusion, and strife, but when we are willing to obey the Holy Spirit, we will find ourselves steadfast, safe, protected, secure, and right where we should be. If nothing else, the pandemic revives an even greater possibility of a clean heart and a steadfast spirit.

The Psalmist says, "[c]reate in me a pure heart, O' God, and renew a steadfast spirit within me. Do not cast me from your presence or take your Holy Spirit from me. Restore to me the joy of your salvation and grant me a willing spirit, to sustain me" (Psalms 51:10-12). A clean heart requires that we move out of our own way and stop blocking our good.

From this moment forward, I will trust the universe. God can do no more for me than God can do through me. I will study. I will pray. I will meditate. I will surround myself with positive people. I will get the rest that I need. I will eat the foods that are nourishing. I will be one with the will that never stops teaching me, one with the will that never stops opening channels of divine ideas, one with the will of infinite creation, one with the will that moves beyond the stress, pain, sickness, and despair of this pandemic and rises with new light, new love, new favor, new awareness, new hope, new victory, new glory of deep listening, with a clean heart that abides by the power of what God.

I decree that I have a willing spirit.

I Have a Superpower of Zeal

It's time to be zealous as Spirit.

I n Titus 2:14, Paul says that Jesus was zealous for good works. You might want good, but are you zealous for it? We can stay limited in our human, physical form, or we can be true to the pure energy of Spirit. As spiritual beings, we can move beyond the boundaries of fear and the confines of mediocrity. As spiritual beings, we can be courageous enough to do more through Spirit than through flesh. Zeal gives us the energy beyond lethargy and laziness to be open and receptive to manifest what really brings us joy. With zeal, we stop judging ourselves by age, experience, opportunity, finances, and other limitations that we place upon our consciousness and instead tap the energy of right ideas, tireless motivation, and divine source.

Jesus told the disciples to stay in the upper room until they were guided by the Holy Spirit. This message is like saying, wait before you act until you are blessed with the zeal of your anointing. The zeal of our anointing is readily available to us. We can tap it here and now. Every channel of God's good is available to us. With zeal, the shackles of limitation fall, and our expectations are raised to attain the miracles we await. With the power of zeal, we touch the presence of God with our hearts and know, really know that God lives in us.

With zeal, we can move forward with energy and enthusiasm, knowing that God will take care of the details. We will be directed to the right things, the right people, the right circumstances, and the right events. With the zeal of exuberance and excitement, whatever we need will be revealed to us when we need to know it.

There are no enemies in God; the pure love of Spirit will devour them so that nothing remains but love. We can longer be mad at our enemies because the pure power of love does not have room for resentment or animosity. There is no room for even our own toxic energy and certainly none for the accumulation of somebody else's stuff.

With the infinite energy of zeal, we can clean our temples so that only our highest consciousness remains. Pure love is a healer. Pure love will neutralize the poison, eradicate the debris, and disinfect any lingering traces of negativity until nothing is left but the pure presence of Spirit.

Jesus said, "[d]estroy this temple, and in three days I will raise it up." But He wasn't talking about the church; he was talking about the temple of his body. He showed us all that he lives with zeal for whatever we need when we need it.

The zeal of Jesus is present in every decision we make, every step we take, every word we speak, and everything we do. Raising the roof up results from deep cleaning, going into the veins and the inner parts of true confession, untangling the roots that have been twisted, eradicating the lies that have been told, washing away the suffering of shame.

Through the power of zeal, we aim, target, and hit the bullseye, releasing old sins to be fully accountable, to allow penetrating power of God to tear down the walls of weakness, wash us in new waters of faith, baptize us in the fullness of grace, and allow our anointing to embrace us, so that we know nothing, breathe nothing, and seek nothing but the pure power of God.

> *I decree that I embrace God with the zeal of my entire being.*

I Have a Superpower of Divine Ideas

It's time to tap divine ideas.

I am a co-creative power of divine ideas, in tune with the eternal flow of Spirit present in everything created. In the book of Genesis, Chapter 1, Verses 21-23, God said, "[l]et the water teem with living creatures, and let birds fly above the earth across the vault of the sky." So, God created every living thing. And God saw that it was good. God blessed them and said, "[b]e fruitful and increase in number and fill the water in the seas, and let the birds increase on the earth." This was the fifth dawning of creation, the pure potential of divine ideas always available to us, teeming, flying, and swarming in the quantum realm of endless possibilities.

The ideas that need to take shape are always present. The answers that we need are always available to us. Even the messiness, confusion, mistakes are all blessings, all part of our superpower of divine ideas. We see the sacredness of ideas in the story of Wag Dodge, who was forced to tap divine ideas during a forest fire in 1949 in Montana. Fifteen firefighters parachuted in and found themselves surrounded by fire moving over six hundred feet per minute. They could not outrun it, so what were they going to do? How would they survive?

Pushed to the edge of his existence, Wag Dodge got an idea. He stopped and lit a fire at his own feet, urging the other firefighters to join him as the fire spread around him. He did the opposite of what would appear logical, believing that if he burned the fuel around him when the fire came, it would not enter the circle of flames already burning, and he would be safe. Unfortunately, no one was willing to step outside the comfort zone of their own limited thinking, so everyone was killed except Wag Dodge. Thirteen hundred acres burned, but Wag Dodge created what is now known and used by all firefighters as an "escape fire." He survived because he trusted a divine idea.

Sometimes it is in the middle of catastrophe, chaos, and confusion that we are not merely blessed with genius but with the courage and capacity to impact the lives of generations to come. As part of an infinite universe of divine ideas that are everywhere present, we always have a superpower available to us, just waiting for us to co-create them into being. But we must be willing to step into the unknown and do something different, be open to a new voice, guided by a new direction, take a new risk.

When we want to access the divine ideas that are always available to us, my team at work closes the door and practices "design thinking." We get a whiteboard. We take different color post-its, and without judging the idea that comes to our minds, we arrange the post-its of the ideas on the board in different categories. I like my colleague Gina to lead this challenge because she is diplomatic and encouraging in leading us all to surrender to the whiteboard as we pour the endless ideas of the universe, using the whiteboard to gather all of our musings together and thereby liberate us all from ownership, pride, or judgment. We continue to re-shuffle and re-categorize the ideas based on those that resonate with the group until we arrive at a select few that will serve our purpose. We let go of ego and flow instead with the freely moving co-creative energy all around us. (For virtual brainstorming, we use an app called MIRO.)

We also like to study spaces where the best creativity takes place. We visited the offices of IDEO, creators of the computer mouse, and one of the largest creative companies in the world. We wanted to see how their workspace supports the free flow of ideas. Every nook of their workplace was a full expression of creative energy. There were many open spaces, inviting others to share them in collaboration, spaces where they could display their ideas and share their genius.

As we sit in our home spaces, we are blessed with a divine opportunity to do things differently, to push past our edges of risk into a future that needs the power of divine ideas. If Wag Dodge had not been in that fire, the world would have lost the technique that has since saved many lives. If we were not forced to communicate and share collective energy and resilience-building habits now, we would lose the power of their contribution in the future.

Yesterday, the thought finally occurred to me that I could experience this lockdown differently. Instead of coming out worse, I can emerge better. The Psalmist says, "the Lord is my Shepherd, I shall not want." I have everything I need. I have no shortage of divine ideas that will bless me, prosper me, and deliver me: there is no limit to God's good.

The First Book of Kings illustrates this universal law in the 17th Chapter, Verses 8-16, when the Prophet Elijah went to Zarephath and asked a starving widow for food. Even though the widow only had a handful of flour in a jar and a little oil in a jug, she shared what she had with Elijah. After she gave, they had food every day, and the flour was not used up, nor did the jug of oil run dry. What we need is always here in the vast idea-swarms around us. Our ideas never stop flowing.

We do not need what someone else has because the Universe is always blessing us with what we need when we need it, always giving us the prosperity of absolute good through our superpower of divine ideas.

I decree the flow of divine ideas here and now.

I Have a Superpower of Obedience – Part 1

It's time to obey God's good.

O ne example of obedience is in Matthew 3:13-16, where the Bible teaches us that Jesus came from Galilee to the Jordan to be baptized by John. But John tried to deter him, saying, "I need to be baptized by you, and do you come to me?" Jesus replied, "Let it be so now; it is proper for us to do this to fulfill all righteousness." Then John obeyed. Water baptism symbolizes a cleansing process—not just the act of washing our sins but the cleansing process of washing our souls.

Today, let us stand in the water with John and Jesus, and if there is anything in your life that you need to cleanse, be obedient and do so right now. The River Jordan, where Jesus was baptized, is the stream of Spirit where we cleanse our sins. We baptize old conditions, old doubts, old worries, old fears, old judgments, old disease, and accept the absolute good of the quantum realm.

The scripture also teaches us that in Matthew 4:18-20, when Jesus was walking by the Sea of Galilee, he saw two brothers, Simon called Peter, and Andrew his brother, casting a net into the sea, for they were fishermen. Then He said to them, 'Follow Me, and I will make you fishers of men.' They immediately left their nets and followed Him." This exchange symbolizes leaving our everyday doubts and worries by being obedient to higher Christ Consciousness. We can leave our nets of fear and follow power. We can leave our nets of ignorance and follow truth. We can leave our nets of lack and follow plenty.

Another lesson of obedience is in John 6:54-58, when Jesus says, "[w]hoever eats My flesh and drinks My blood has eternal life, and I will raise him up at the last day." When we take communion of the bread and water of Christ metaphysically with obedience, we are infused with the Spirit.

I decree that I am obedient to the Absolute Good of Spirit.

I Have a Superpower
of Obedience – Part 2

It's time to be obedient to the I AM.

I n John 8:57-58, Jesus was asked, "[y]ou are not yet fifty years old and have You seen Abraham?" Jesus said, "[m]ost assuredly, I say to you, before Abraham was, I AM." We must be obedient in embracing the I AM as who we are. I AM is God's affirmation as humanity; I AM is Jehovah, the indwelling Christ, the true spiritual man God made in His image and likeness.

The outer, manifest man is the offspring of the I AM or inner spiritual man. By use of I AM, we make conscious union with Spirit. When we say I AM, we embody the kingdom of the heavens within us.

In John 11:23-25, Jesus tells Martha, "[y]our brother will rise again." And Martha said to Him, "I know that he will rise again in the resurrection on the last day." Jesus said to her, "I am the resurrection and the life. He who believes in Me, though he may die, he shall live."

We must be obedient to the power of Christ consciousness that resurrects new awareness in us and evolves from our old ways and modes of thinking. Say "Jesus lives in me." No matter how difficult life may appear, I know Jesus is resurrected in my heart, and his Spirit lives in me. Jesus said, "isn't it written in your own law that you are gods" (John 10:34). We rise from the dead. We are resurrected through the God in us.

In John 13:34-35, it is written that Jesus said, "a new commandment I give to you, that you love one another; as I have loved you, that you also love one another. By this, all will know that you are My disciples if you have love for one another." These are the parting words he left them with, one of the last lessons before he departed.

We must be obedient in loving one another and liberate ourselves right now from whatever disconnects us from the power of Jesus. Let your enemies go.

In John 14:14, Jesus says, "whatever you ask in My name, that I will do, that the Father may be glorified in the Son. If you ask anything in My name, I will do it." We must be obedient and ask God for what we want. In the asking, we receive the Holy Spirit as our guide (John 20:22). Asking is not just for material things but for a shift in consciousness.

In Matthew 28:19-20, Jesus says, "Go therefore and make disciples of all the nations, baptizing them in the name of the Father and of the Son and of the Holy Spirit, teaching them to observe all things that I have commanded you; and lo, I am with you always, even to the end of the age."

We must be obedient, not in proselytizing or trying to convert people into our way of thinking, but obedient in shining the energy, power, and presence of God as us. Then, if students are drawn to you, you can share the Word with deference and humility.

Anoint yourself with Jesus' living water. Baptize your consciousness in the name of the Father, the Son, and the Holy Spirit. Realize that Jesus is with you always—even to the end of time. Do not worry about a thing because Spirit will shine from your body, live in your heart, and speak from your lips.

I decree that I am obedient
to the wisdom of God.

I Have a Superpower of Storytelling

It's time to tell a new story.

Our lives tell a story, and the more we live that story, the less daring we are to deviate from the script. But the scripts that we live and read lines from are based on events around us. The law of storytelling opens our hearts to realize that our experiences do not limit us but are opportunities to move forward.

We can always tell a new story. Even when we are locked in, the co-creative power of God is never locked out. We are never limited by our stories; we are transformed because of them. We don't have to lock ourselves into a life with the same cast of characters, the same dialogue, the same plot, and the same chapters that we keep living over and over. We can tell a new story.

The law of storytelling not only supports how our stories have given us the ability to grow, inspire, motivate, and excel but also the ability to move beyond the confines of the appearances that we thought limited us so that we seize our ability to reinvent ourselves as the images and likenesses of God that we are.

The law of storytelling requires us to start a new chapter, empower new characters, and build new strength. What if the story that we told ourselves was not about the past, not about the mistakes we made—not about something we did wrong or how someone wronged us—but about a magnificence liberated from a mind tied to the flesh one fully aware of its supernatural abilities? Great achievement is always preceded by preparation of some sort. Telling a new story ends the pity party, realizing what we thought was bad is really a blessing: God calling us to reclaim life in a new way.

I decree the power of my new story.

I Have a Superpower
of the Word

It's time to be the Word of God.

How do you ignore, undermine, marginalize, dispel, second-guess the Word in you? This negativity bias or inner critic shows up in the best circumstances to tell us that we are not worthy, that we are less than, that we are not good enough. Some of us may hear the voice so distinctly and judge ourselves so severely that we view everything said to us through that lens.

One minute we hear the Word of God, and we are filled with the Spirit; the next minute, we are deflated by the passing comment from a coworker or an associate or a spouse or a parent, torturing ourselves over something they said. What others say is not essential. Our embrace of the power of spiritual law depends on what we tell ourselves. Jesus dealt with negativity bias a different way; he said, get thee behind me, Satan.

When the devil stood before Jesus in the wilderness, tempting him to turn the stones into bread, Jesus answered, "[m]an shall not live by bread alone, but by every word that proceedeth out of the mouth of God." When Satan tempted the Master to cast himself down from the pinnacle of the temple, and Jesus said, you shall not tempt the Lord thy God. When Satan offered him temptation in the form of worldly glory, Jesus replied, "Get thee hence, Satan." The appearance of lack, limitation, evil, sin, shame only has the power we give.

What we tell ourselves reflects what we see, what we co-create in the world. We imagine the worst-case scenario. We jump to conclusions. We attribute things to ourselves through speculation that have nothing to do with us. We dwell on the glass half empty instead of half full. But we can turn our inner critic into an inner coach by realizing the unlimited power of Spirit always operating in us. We can tell ourselves the right thing and energize the invisible ethers, the divine energy, the pure substance that is all around us, the vibrations of God, the Spirit in which we live and move and have our being.

Everything we say is truth spoken to power because our consciousness cannot distinguish between what we say and what we want. Our feeling of lack which hardens into jealousy, is not Truth. The imaginary limitations that we create to impose artificial barriers between ourselves and the completion of our goals are not Truth.

What we perceive as our bank accounts or our wealth or our money is not Truth because it expands and multiplies or decreases based on how we choose to perceive it. Our jobs are not Truth; they are but one aspect of the manifestation of the world that we CHOOSE to speak into existence. Telling ourselves the right thing is using the divine energy that we were given as a catalyst to mold, shape, summon, command, build, uplift, or create what we WANT to experience in our lives.

What we say to ourselves is not just our decree; it is our consciousness. Our words manifest what we speak. The Book of John, Chapter 1: Verse 1 says, "In the beginning was the Word, and the Word was with God, and the Word was God."

Similarly, Job says in Chapter 22, Verse 28, you shall decree a thing, and it shall be established unto thee. Jesus was great at simplifying things, he just said, ask, and you shall receive. Our Word is our intention. Our Word is our Vision. Our words reach beyond the appearance of now, stirred by Spirit.

What we tell ourselves is the Dynamic Energy of our Faith, blessing us to trust in the dynamic power of the universe, the Magnificent Force of Creation constantly creating itself, the Breakthrough that we have been waiting for.

The law of Word, what we tell ourselves, allows us to move through the portal more connected to source than we have ever been, to speak a new truth for ourselves, and to leave the Satan that we created behind, to speak in such a way that we obtain the prize. As 1 Corinthians 9:24-27 says, everyone who competes for the prize is temperate in all things; they do it to obtain a perishable crown, but we for an imperishable crown.

I decree the power of the Word.

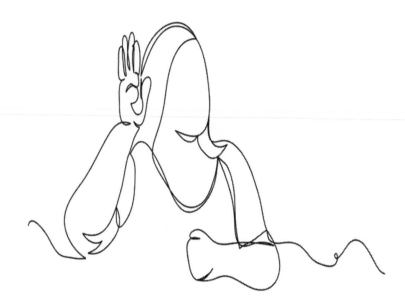

I Affirm the Power in Me

It's time to affirm our blessings.

I n Ephesians Chapters 1 and 2, we learn about the spiritual gifts that we have been given. Today, we take the opportunity to affirm them.

I AM CHOSEN TO BE HOLY AND BLAMELESS.
I AM PREDESTINED TO THE PRAISE
OF GLORIOUS GRACE.
I AM REDEEMED THROUGH HIS BLOOD.
I AM FORGIVEN OF ALL SINS.
I AM LAVISHED WITH GOD'S RICHES.

I AM FULFILLED WITH THE UNITY
OF ALL THINGS IN HEAVEN AND EARTH
IN THE CONSCIOUSNESS OF CHRIST.
I AM GOD'S PLAN, WORKED OUT IN CONFORMITY
WITH THE PURPOSE OF HIS WILL.
I AM THE MESSAGE OF TRUTH.
I AM CHILD OF THE RULER OF THE KINGDOM OF THE
AIR, THE SPIRIT WHO IS NOW AT WORK.
BY GOD'S GRACE, I HAVE BEEN SAVED.
I AM RAISED UP WITH CHRIST AND SEATED WITH HIM,
A WILLING AUDIENCE AND WITNESS TO HIS GRACE.
I AM GOD'S HANDIWORK, CREATED IN CHRIST JESUS
TO DO GOOD WORKS, WHICH GOD PREPARED
IN ADVANCE FOR ME TO DO.
FOR THROUGH HIM, WE BOTH HAVE ACCESS
TO THE FATHER BY ONE SPIRIT.

I AM NO LONGER A STRANGER.
I AM THE CORNERSTONE.
I AM THE BUILDING JOINED TOGETHER.
I AM THE HOLY TEMPLE.
I AM THE DWELLING
IN WHICH GOD LIVES BY HIS SPIRIT.

The Father is With Me

It's time to go to the Father.

I n Deuteronomy 32:6, the Deuteronomist asks: Is he not your Father, your Creator, who made you and formed you? If you study the scripture, it is not until Jesus is born that we begin to see God as Father of us all, which simply means that God will see us through regardless of what we experience. The scripture says when you pray, go into your room, close the door and pray to your Father, who is unseen. Then your Father, who sees what is done in secret, will reward you. And when you pray, do not keep on babbling like pagans, for they think they will be heard because of their many words. Do not be like them, for your Father knows what you need before you ask him. (Matthew 6:6-13).

In Matthew 18:19, Jesus teaches us to come together, and the Father will reward us: "Again, truly I tell you that if two of you on earth agree about anything they ask for, it will be done for them by my Father in heaven."

Luke 12:32 says our Father is pleased to give us the kingdom. The Law of the Father makes clear (Matthew 19:29) whatever we give or sacrifice to the Father will return a hundredfold: "And everyone who has left houses or brothers or sisters or father or mother or wife or children or fields for my sake will receive a hundred times as much and will inherit eternal life."

Where is the Father?

Jesus says He is always in us and that we can always return to the Father from the far country of disconnection. Luke 15:20-22 says no matter what we do, our Father's love is unconditional, that he will put the best robe on us, put a ring on our fingers and sandals on our feet and kill the fatted calf to feed us. Wherever we go, we return to a consciousness of absolute good. Luke 15:31 says The Father said: "you are always with me, and everything I have is yours."

I decree all that the Father has is mine.

I am God Expressing as Me

It's time to know God's grace.

I have certain experiences as a woman in a body racialized as black because I share the tradition of ancestors similarly situated, who allow me to be and experience the full power of who I AM. I carry the insight of my ancestors in the flesh and the Spirit, but I also am the infinite depth and wisdom of God. I AM THAT I AM, the God of Grace, the God of a Way out of no way, the God of decency, respect, and soul that reverberates and expresses as a woman of infinite creative power. We can be greater than who we ever imagined in the flesh because we are God in the Spirit. *We need to recognize the power of who we are: no one in the flesh is better or worse than who we are.*

In *Practical Metaphysics*, Eric Butterworth says, "The difference between Jesus and you and I was not one of the mere manner of his birth, it was not because of some special dispensation, it was not just because of some mere potentiality that was in him but not in others—the difference was in *his awareness of that potential*." Are you aware of your pure potential? Jesus' ministry was based on the fact that we can do even greater things. The heart of Jesus' teachings was not the depravity of man but the divinity of man. His ministry was devoted to the "repeatability of the Christ."

"Nothing shall be impossible unto you," he said. "There are the things that I do, you can do, too, and greater things shall you do if you have faith" (John 14:12). Christ is the God possibility within every person. We are created in God's own image and likeness (Genesis 1:26, 27). The image is you and as God sees you, and the likeness is that which you must work out in your consciousness, body, and soul. In other words, as we say so often, within you is the unborn possibility of limitless life. This is the image, and yours is the privilege of giving birth to it.

I decree that God is the possibility within me.

I Stand on the Shoulders of My Ancestors

It's time to stand on the shoulders of grace.

Despite what goes on in the world, we have an extraordinary power that resides in us, a power that enables us to pull back the curtain on the appearances of things and experience the true power of what is. We need to remember that the human potential in us is divine. What does that mean? We are all the All-ness of the Infinite Mind. As Paul says, awake now, that sleeper, that Christ may shine upon you (Ephesians 5:14). Awaken to the power that God is expressing as you. Awaken to the truth that the Universe is telling through you. Awaken to the pure potential of your own divinity.

Our circle of truth is not to beg but to remember that we are the whole being of God and that within us radiates the truth that keeps pouring, keeps healing, keeps manifesting, keeps blessing, keeps restoring, keeps uplifting, keeps rescuing us through the conduction of our souls beyond the world.

I decree that my ancestors keep blessing me.

We Begin Again

It's time to start over.

We are given the rare opportunity to begin again. Now is the time to get rid of policies that allow putting hundreds of children in jail, that support the killing of others in the guise of capital punishment, that allow police brutality, that encourages the loss of lives through the spread of diseases like COVID-19, that denounce diversity and inclusion training, that help the rich but not the poor. Before he passed, Representative John Lewis uplifted 'satya,' or truth, to expose the generations of racism in which our country is rooted. After more than 400 years of oppression in America, Black and brown men, women, and children continue to be targeted.

Fortunately, there are leaders in all of us. We extend our prayers to the leadership in us, which is the most difficult to achieve.

We are all called to be better, assume responsibility, and make this world a better place than the one we arrived in.

We are the potential of perfection within, expressing what needs to be done. The power of prayer is not in asking but in realizing that we always have the power present within us, that we can always release the potential that has never been expressed before. We need to begin to see ourselves, as Paul says, not in a mirror darkly, but face-to-face (1 Corinthians 13:12), as part of the divine process.

You have a God potential within you, and you must respond every time life presents you with a challenge of any kind, shape, or form; life is asking you, "Who do you think you are?"

How do you respond? "I AM who I AM."

"I AM the heir of the living God. I can deal with this, and I know that I will succeed. I will do it easily, and I will do it well." When we begin to deal with life as triumph, life takes on new meaning.

I decree that we can be better than ever before.

We Have the Power to Manifest the Change We Seek

It's time to transform.

As we deal with all of our challenges, the lies, and attacks on the democracy of our country by the racism, hatred, greed, and selfishness, we need to tap the power that we have to bring about change and transformation. In *Practical Metaphysics*, Eric Butterworth teaches us that the secret of demonstrating that we desire is not something in the material world. *No, the secret of demonstration is the Christ in us.* Eric says that this means realizing that "the whole oak tree is established in the acorn." The absolute good is in the soul, or as Jesus taught, the kingdom of God is within you.

The secret of demonstration is to realize that we are so much more than what we seem. We have not merely scratched the surface of our full potential. We think we are the oak tree, but we are still in the infancy of the acorn.

We have the power to manifest the change that we seek. We may not always know how our desires will be expressed, but we will experience the change we seek. The power in us is greater than what is in the world. We never see in the flesh what is happening in the Spirit. The Divine Mind of Spirit is within us, and we are within it. Our good, our power, our joy, our health, our prosperity is not outside of us, it is within us. We have the power to bring about the change that will bless everyone, recognize that we should take pride in all groups, and level the playing field for those who have been denied support for so long.

We have the power to make sure that our voices are heard. Most of us have been absorbed in the immediate needs that we have for ourselves, but it is time to be more diligent—to make sure that we are doing what needs to be done to protect our rights and to put only people in office who guarantee the protection of the rights, prosperity, health, and success of everyone.

We step up to the plate of our own greatness. We wake up to the power of God as us. We pray together for and receive guidance. God is expressing absolute good at the point at which we are, and every prayer is heard.

> *I decree the change and transformation that we need.*

RESOURCES

Braden, Gregg. *The Science of Self-Empowerment: Awakening the New Human Story.* Carlsbad: Hay House, 2017.

Brown, Edward Espe. *The Tassajara Bread Book.* Boston: Shambhala Books, 2009.

Butterworth, Eric. *Practical Metaphysics: A New Insight in Truth.* Unity Village: Unity Books, 2017.

———. *The Creative Life: Seven Keys to Your Inner Genius.* New York: Jeremy P. Tarcher/Putnam, 2001.

———. *The Universe is Calling: Opening to the Divine Through Prayer.* San Francisco: Harper Collins e-Books, 2010.

———. *Discover the Power Within You: A Guide to the Unexplored Depths Within.* San Francisco: Harper Collins e-Books, 2009.

———. *Breaking the Ten Commandments: Discover the Deeper meaning,* Unity Village: Unity Books, 2011.

Dispenza, Dr. Joe, *Becoming Supernatural: How Common People Are Doing the Uncommon,* Carlsbad: Hay House, 2017.

———. *Breaking the Habit of Being Yourself: How to Lose Your Mind and Create a New One,* Carlsbad: Hay House, 2012.

Fillmore, Charles. *Mysteries of Genesis.* Unity Village: Unity Books, 1998.

Fulghum, Robert L. *All I Really Need to Know I Learned in Kindergarten: Uncommon Thoughts on Common Things.* New York, Ballentine, 2004.

Gibran, Kahlil. *The Prophet.* New York: Alfred A. Knopf, 1999.

Goldsmith, Joel. *Seek Ye First.* Georgia: Acropolis Books, 1972.

———. *Realization of Oneness: The Practice of Spiritual Healing.* Secaucus: Citadel, 1974.

Hubbard, Barbara Marx, *Conscious Evolution: Awakening the Power of Our Social Potential.* Novato: New World Library, 2015.

Kaufman, Samahria Lyte. "Love Wins." *Handbook for the Heart.* Edited by Richard Carlson and Benjamin Shield. Boston: Little Brown & Company, 1996.

Landone, Brown. *Soul Catalysts and How to Use Them.* London: L.N. Fowler & Co., 1939.

Loving, Cecilia B. *Prayers for Those Standing on the Edge of Greatness.* Brooklyn: Myrtle Tree Press, 2009.

Painter, Nell Irvin, *Sojourner Truth: A Life, A Symbol.* New York: W.W. Norton & Company, Inc., 1996.

Ponder, Catherine. *The Prospering Power of Love.* Unity Village: Unity Books, 1966.

Salzberg, Sharon. *Lovingkindness: The Revolutionary Art of Happiness.* Boston: Shambhala Books, 2011.

Thich Nhat Hanh. *Going Home: Jesus and Buddha as Brothers.* New York: Riverhead Books, 1999.

West, Georgiana Tree. *Prosperity's Ten Commandments.* Unity Village: Unity Books, 1944.

Yogananda, Paramahansa. *Autobiography of a Yogi.* Los Angeles: Self-Realization Fellowship, 1998.

ABOUT THE
AUTHOR

Cecilia B. Loving is an award-winning speaker, diversity, equity, accessibility, and inclusion (DEAI) thought leader, consultant, and author.

Her work in restorative justice, storytelling, inclusive leadership, racial inclusion, mindfulness, and well-being helps redefine the importance of self-care and self-empowerment to create a positive and holistic environment for everyone. Her experience in uplifting the opportunity that DEAI presents for the success of organizations includes both the private and public sectors.

Cecilia has a Juris Doctor from NYU School of Law, a Master of Divinity from NY Theological Seminary, a BFA from Howard University, and an MFA in Theatre Management from UCLA's School of Theatre, Film, and Television. She is also certified in Diversity and Inclusion by Cornell University School of Industrial and Labor Relations and Yale University School of Management.

With over 20 years of experience as a lawyer in private law firms, a background in Human Rights Law, leadership as an ordained minister, experience providing DEAI leadership for both businesses and government agencies, Cecilia combines legal, analytical, and strategic skills to co-create a positive and holistic work environment.

She is a winner of the National Diversity Council's 2021 Top 100 Diversity Officers Award; the New York City Department of Citywide Administrative Services' 2021 Innovation Award for FDNY's Inclusive Culture Strategy; Lawline's Top Women Faculty of 2020 Award; the City Bar Association's 2020 Diversity and Inclusion Champion Award; ABC News' First Responder Friday Award, as well as several other awards.

Rev. Loving, also known as #LovingFactor, is a certified Circle Keeper and leader of healing circles, especially those supporting racial inclusion and equity.

She has authored several books, including but not limited to the following books.

The Power of Inclusion: Meditating with Compassion,
Healing with Generosity, Leading with Love

Unbroken Circles: Holding Space, Healing Harm,
and Transcending Edges

God is a Lawyer Too

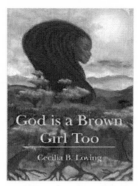

God is a Brown Girl Too

Prayers for Those Standing on the Edge of Greatness

Seeing Myself as God Sees Me

Made in the USA
Middletown, DE
24 June 2021